How to Thrive at Architecture School

A Student Guide

© RIBA Publishing, 2020

Published by RIBA Publishing, 66 Portland Place, London, W1B 1AD

ISBN 978 1 85946 908 8

The right of Neil Spiller to be identified as the Author of this Work has been asserted
in accordance with the Copyright, Designs and Patents Act 1988 sections 77 and 78.

British Library Cataloguing-in-Publication Data
A catalogue record for this book is available from the British Library.

Commissioning Editor: Alex White
Assistant Editor: Clare Holloway
Production: Sarah-Louise Deazley
Designed and typeset by The First 47
Printed and bound by L.E.G.O. spa
Cover image: Muneeb Kahn, London South Bank University (front)
             James Dalley, Mackintosh School of Architecture (back)

While every effort has been made to check the accuracy and quality of the
information given in this publication, neither the Author nor the Publisher accept
any responsibility for the subsequent use of this information, for any errors or
omissions that it may contain, or for any misunderstandings arising from it.

All quotes from external sources in the book were made
in private correspondence with the author.

www.ribapublishing.com

How to Thrive at Architecture School

A Student Guide

RIBA ☗ Publishing

Neil Spiller

VII   About the Author
VII   Acknowledgements

INTRODUCTION

1   So, you want to be an architect?

PART 1: UNDERGRADUATE

5   **Getting to school**
5   What is architectural practice?
5   Pre-application: modes of study and alternative routes
17   Selecting and applying to schools of architecture
21   Preparing for interview: making a portfolio
25   The interview itself
26   Offers, results and clearing

31   **First year**
33   The fundamentals
40   First-term drawing, modelling and scaling
45   The first building brief: becoming a proper architect
50   Images for your first building proposal
51   The first serious crit: a user's guide
54   How to write an essay
56   The end of first year
59   Mental health and managing stress

63   **Second and third year**
63   The difference between first year and second year
64   What will second year look like?
66   Second year briefs and skills development
70   Why is history important?
75   Why is theory important?
78   Technology and the future
82   Landscape and reducing the carbon footprint:
     greening your building
86   Third year (full-time) or fourth year (part-time)

PART 2: POSTGRADUATE

93 **Year(s) out and working in an office**
93 Preparing for year(s) out
95 Applying for jobs
96 Preparing your portfolio
98 Deferrals and academic currency
99 PEDR
99 Office life
102 Preparing to return to university and picking your route
106 Part 2 course options

111 **MArch and Part 2**
111 Starting your master's in architecture (Part 2)
113 History, theory and futures
116 Realising architecture
122 Looking to the future: architectural speculation
125 Being an architecture student in a post-digital world
133 The architecture of augmented reality
134 The architectural uses of AI
136 Finishing Part 2

PART 3: PART 3

141 **Studying abroad**
141 Participating in prolonged study abroad

149 **Part 3**
149 Finding a post-Part 2 job, and Part 3
151 Part 3
154 Continuing professional development
155 Completing Part 3

157 Appendix 1 (Useful resources for financial matters, mental wellbeing, diversity, professional development and others)
162 Appendix 2 (RIBA Plan of Work)
165 Image Credits
166 Index

About the Author

Neil Spiller is Editor of AD and is founding Director of the AVATAR Group (Advanced Virtual and Technological Architectural Research). He has been Hawksmoor Chair of Architecture and Landscape and Deputy Pro Vice-Chancellor of the University of Greenwich, London. Prior to this he was Vice-Dean and Graduate Director of Design at the Bartlett School of Architecture, University College London. His own work has been exhibited internationally and featured in many collections worldwide. His books include *Cyberreader: Critical Writings of the Digital Era* (2002), *Digital Dreams* (1998), *Visionary Architecture – Blueprints of the Modern Imagination* (2006), *Digital Architecture Now* (2008), *Educating Architects* (2014) and *Surrealism and Architecture – A Blistering Romance* (2016). Spiller is also recognised internationally for his paradigm shifting contribution to architectural drawing, discourse, research/experiment and teaching. Prior to becoming Editor of AD, he has guest edited eight editions including the influential and pioneering *Architects in Cyberspace* (1995) and *Architects in Cyberspace II* (1998).

Acknowledgements

I would like to thank Helen Castle, Publishing Director, at the RIBA for having the original idea for this book and thinking that I would have the right "tone" for it. I would also like to thank Alex White, Commissioning Editor, for his steadfast and supportive work on this project and all the employees of the RIBA from many disparate areas/expertise who have helped in the production of this book and/or provided quotes and resources. My thanks also go to the practitioners, academics and schools of architecture that have been involved with the project quotation-wise and image-wise.

So, you want to be an architect?

Architecture is everywhere – and it's exciting, full of possibilities. Civilisations are marked by their buildings and structures, providing historical and cultural significance to the places upon which they are built. Individually, buildings characterise and shape our daily lives; collectively, they form a vast repository of centuries of human ingenuity, expression and beauty. Yet all of these forms began with a spark in somebody who decided to enter a classroom with designs of their own to add to the wonders of human history.

To be an architect takes years of preparation and study. This preparation starts well before architecture school. It starts on the day you decide that you want to be an architect. This book is a guide to the process: it will help you see what's coming, why it's coming, and how it contributes to the build-up of your architectural knowledge and skills.

It takes creativity, ambition and an ability to maximise and respond quickly to opportunities when they show themselves. You will develop the skills to be spatially dexterous, numerate, literate and legally astute, and understand how things go together in terms of teams, materials, contracts, commissions and human networks, while negotiating the virtual in all its current and future forms.

Students will move on to practise around the world, having diverse careers; some teaching architecture, some forming their own firms. You can work at the domestic scale or a larger scale, including the urban design of cities. Or you could even move into theatre set design, game design, or exhibition design and curation.

This book will help you prepare applications to universities, show you how to select appropriate schools, how to prepare a portfolio, how to conduct yourself in a interview for a place, right through to graduation as a fully fledged architect, one step at a time. It will introduce you to the key concepts of architectural training, critical tactics and protocols of architectural representation and production, architectural styles, dogmas and doctrines, and architectural expressions and ways of seeing and describing. It includes illustrations from top Royal Institute of British Architects (RIBA)-validated architecture schools and shows the great diversity of what has and might constitute architecture.

This book is a primer for the next decade of your architectural life. Keep it with you!

0.1
University of Edinburgh, Ruth McNickle, Tilling the Prado, Year 2 MArch.
A clever image of the building proposal showing various views, sections and context, collaged into a hybrid drawing and virtual model.

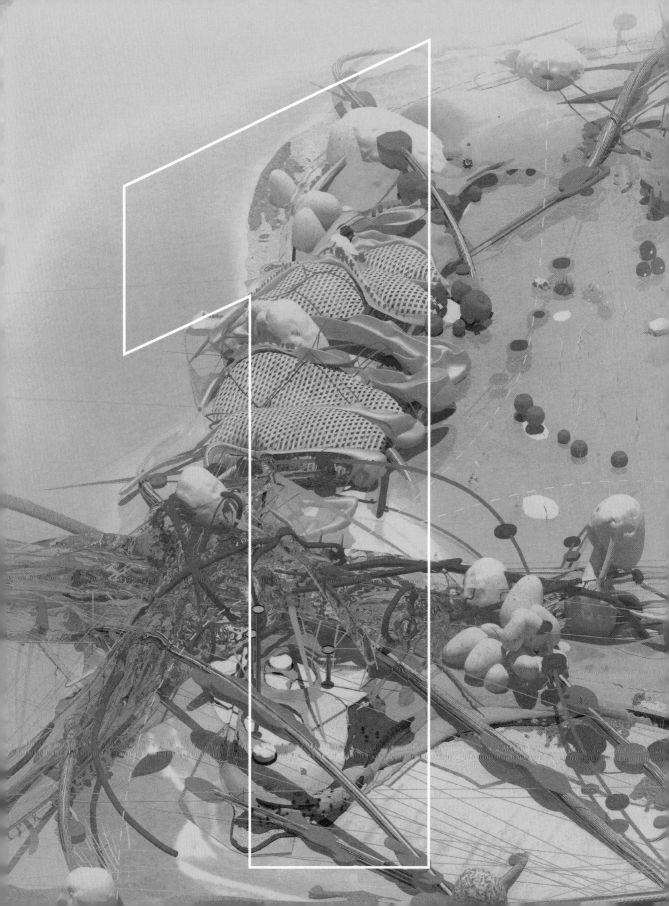

5   **Getting to school**

31   **First year**

63   **Second and third year**

UNDERGRADUATE

Getting to school

You already know who you are. You might like making your own clothes, drawing, modelling, painting, writing prose or poetry, or a mixture of all these. You might already be creative with computers, or wonder about buildings and cities and how they are made. You might wonder about the impact they have on people. You might have an architect in your family, or you might never have met one. Perhaps numerous members of your family and friends have been to university, or you may have no immediate friends and family who've been in higher education.

Whatever else is true, the first thing is you must do is actively decide to study as an architect. Then, you can begin planning. As Dr Harriet Harriss, Dean of Pratt Institute School of Architecture in New York, reminds us: 'The first year of an architecture degree isn't simply the first step towards a career in architectural practice, but the ultimate multidisciplinary experience offered in higher education, exposing students to the natural, formal, social and applied sciences, not just the humanities.'

What is architectural practice?

Architectural practice is providing professional services in connection with the design, construction, extension, conservation, restoration or alteration of a building or group of buildings. This includes (but is not limited to):

- preliminary studies
- planning and land-use planning to ensure proposals are in line with planning regulations and urban plans, and urban design
- designs including models and drawings
- detailed construction drawings, written specifications of materials, and technical documentation
- coordination of technical documentation prepared by others (consulting engineers, urban planners, landscape architects and other specialist consultants)
- construction economics
- contract administration
- inspection of construction
- project management.

Pre-application: modes of study and alternative routes

Before applying to architecture school, you should research the various avenues into practice and speak to people already practising to ensure you're prepared and informed when making that decision.

1.1
University of Dundee Year 1 study trip to Villa Savoye, Poissy, France. Architecture students should experience a wide range of buildings around the world. The field trip is a vitally important element of architecture school. It is also good for student cohort bonding, and it can be a lot of fun.

1.2
University of Brighton, Edmund Morgan, Experiencing Architecture, Year 1. First-year architectural courses get students to consider the body in relation to architectural space, and this can involve making and experimenting with all sorts of measuring and recording devices, and even clothing.

A common piece of advice given to those interested in pursuing architecture is to undertake A Levels in physics, chemistry and maths. Victoria Farrow, course leader for BA Architecture at Birmingham School of Architecture and Design, and first-year leader, says this advice is still pervasive and misguided: 'I continue to strive to disentangle the myth that you need maths and physics to be an architect or to study architecture. This is not the case – or at least, not any more. To study architecture you need energy, enthusiasm, a passion for design and exploration of your ideas and a drive to discover.'

In reality, it doesn't matter what qualifications you take pre-architecture school – the key is to do well. Universities like you to be able to prove you are competent in maths and English at GCSE level. Some universities like you to have a second language qualification at GCSE level. For architectural education, it is wise to have studied art, which is more appreciated by most universities than design technology. Try to pick a broad range of GCSEs, and sixth-form study encompassing creative as well as more empirical and humanities subjects.

The architectural profession is very diverse, varying according to situation, scale of work, commerciality, ethical beliefs, conceptual dogmatic preoccupations and often stylistic habits. It is important to understand this diversity of practice and ideas. Practices include a wide range of scales, from small offices working in a countryside setting on house extensions or conservation projects, to – at the other end of the spectrum – large international firms working on big commercial towers, airports and cultural buildings. Practices can range in size from one-person 'sole practitioners' to large corporations with over a thousand employees. It can be valuable to understand the experiences in different types of architectural office at differing scales. Talk to architects about what they do on a daily basis, as well as talking to them about their architectural education.

Architectural education is about building the ability to solve spatial problems, and the nature of these problems and opportunities will change over the years. A good architectural education gives a student the confidence, skills and intellectual dexterity to operate as an architect, no matter how practice, technology and the procurement of architecture changes. This mental agility and the ability to laterally think through an architectural solution are crucial.

Talking to architectural educators and academics often provides an alternative insight, as their take on studying to be an architect can differ radically from a mid-career architect in a commercial office. Dr Harriet Harriss describes the wider benefits of an education as an architect: 'Rather than thinking the only goal of architecture is to design buildings, students should be encouraged to experiment with the processes as much as the outcomes, and to see all aspects of the curriculum (from lectures and seminars to live projects and studio work) as intrinsically connected and of equal value and importance.'

1.3
University of Strathclyde, Law Yik Yung, The Fun Complex, Year 4.
Architectural students are encouraged to develop projects that become more complex as their training advances. By the time they get to postgraduate/ master's level they should be testing the limits of the discipline.

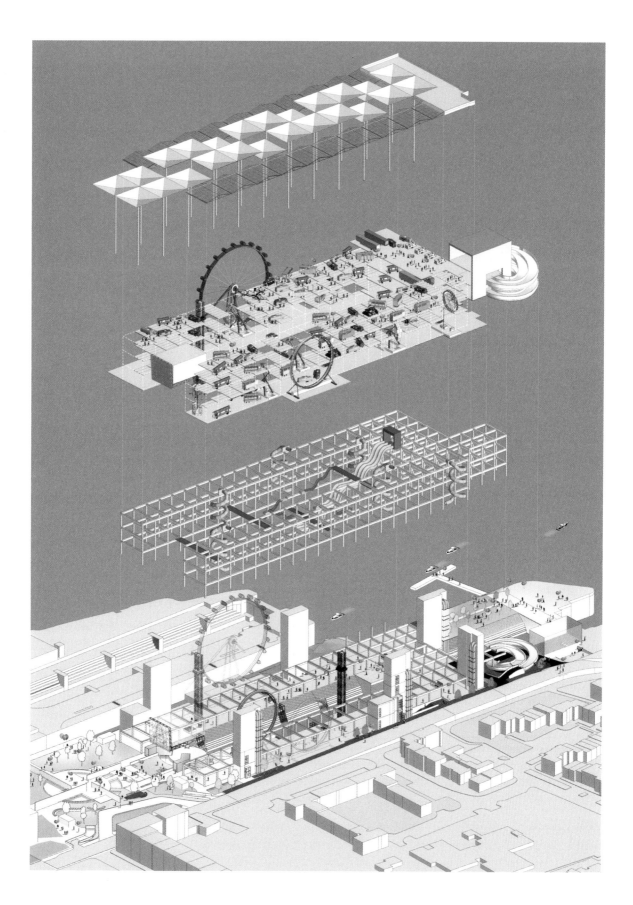

1.4
University of Greenwich, Sarah Brooke,
Repository for the Unclaimed Dead,
Year 2.
**Students are encouraged to use all
different types of media and become
proficient in analogue as well as digital
techniques. The physical model is
vitally important as a method of design,
but also as a means of communication
with laypeople.**

Schools of architecture tend to be incredibly open institutions and should
welcome any approach by a future architecture student. Make contact
with your local school of architecture and, if you're interested in what a
lesson might look like, you can even ask to sit in on tutorials or attend a
lecture. Schools of architecture will hold open days or taster days, which
are worth attending. These events will help you get a feel for a school and
help you decide where to apply. Taster days enable prospective students
to experience studio teaching, view and use facilities and work with staff,
which helps applicants understand the feeling of being in, and contributing
to, design studio and the culture of the school generally.

In June most UK architecture schools have an end-of-year show,
showcasing the best student work of that academic year, and these are
open to attend. They provide insight into the differences between schools
and their signature styles. In particular, observing the first-year work
can reveal how skills are taught and embedded. Schools often produce
extravagant catalogues to accompany their end-of-year show. If you
compare these, you'll notice that some are more technical, while others are
more artful and speculative. Consider what sort of architect you might wish
to be, and whether any of the schools notably match your interests.

All universities and architecture schools have websites and social media
feeds. The vitality and contemporaneity with which they broadcast events

1.5
University of Strathclyde
end-of-year show.
The shows held at the end of the
academic year in June or July are great
opportunities to see the best output
from a school's students – you can tell
a lot about a school from its
end-of-year show.

and lectures can reflect the ambition and liveliness of a school. Public lectures are often made freely available online and offer invaluable insights into the latest trends and ideas being explored at schools. Many students also understand the importance of social media and feature their studio work online. Instagram, Twitter and Facebook have become common places for students to record and showcase their activities on the course, including the design development process, work placements and also studio projects for final presentation. Some universities use student blogs on their websites to market their course to prospective students. These can be great tools for inspiration and getting an idea of the work you could go on to produce at architecture school.

While it may seem daunting, try to talk to current architectural students at these events, as most will be more than willing to share their experiences. Ask them about their workload, studio conditions, technical support, computing provision and tutors' attitudes – and, most importantly, how the course is taught. This will give you an idea of day-to-day life and what to expect.

All universities, including architecture schools, are subject to a growing number of benchmarking processes and metrics, to give prospective students more information. These include teaching and research excellence framework results, league table positions and so on, and they offer insight into the quality of courses. However, it is worth noting that there are schools in the architecture league table for example that don't do RIBA-accredited courses, so you should always dig deeper.

Some schools have a Part 1 (undergraduate), Part 2 (postgraduate) and Part 3 (advanced diploma) course, while others run Parts 1 and 2, or even just Part 2. Ensure you know the make-up of the student body at each school you are interested in. Consider whether you want to study in a completely undergraduate peer group, or if you might benefit from having postgraduate students around for advice, informal mentoring and experience.

Examine which mode of study – part-time, full-time or apprenticeship – would best suit you, your finances and your ambitions. This means understanding the anatomy of the courses you are picking (see Table 1).

1.6
University of Dundee,
Year 2 studio model.
Students are encouraged to make swift and numerous sketch models to test out spatial ideas. They should not be precious about these models, as speed and ideas are most important.

TABLE 1: COMPARING FOUNDATION PROGRAMMES*

Routes and Stages of Qualification	RIBA Foundation in Architecture	Full time
Notes	Delivered in partnership between RIBA and Oxford Brookes University	Based on research about Built Environment Foundation, International Foundation & Foundation in Arts programmes in general
Attributes:		
Geographic location of student	Anywhere in the EEA	Living in or near a University
Cost	No cost to student	9,250/a (Unless HEFE funded)
Prerequisite	No prerequisite. Application; Interview	varies
Programme co-requirements	Working in practice (Oxford Brookes will partner in arranging)	None
Independent learning	Yes. Students have broad opportunity for brief interpretation	This would vary between Universities
Personal Tutor	Yes. Teacher with Arts/ Architecture teaching experience. Regular meetings	Class teacher (group size varies)
Contact time at University /examination	7 days/year	Full time (min of 3 days/ week in semester)
Freedom to shift between practices	YES	N/A
Duration of study	1 year	1 year
Academic workload (outside contact hrs)	20 hrs/week	20 hrs/week
Award & Accreditation	Merit grade offers direct entry to RIBA Studio Certificate and Eligibility to apply for FT with portfolio	Merit grade offers Eligibility to apply to RIBA Studio Certificate and to apply for FT with appropriate portfolio
Part 3 (only relevant during or after Part 2)	N/A	N/A

Credit: Dr Maria Faraone
* Programme under development.

TABLE 1: COMPARING PART 1 PROGRAMMES

Routes and Stages of Qualification	RIBA Studio Certificate	Apprenticeship	Part time	Full time
Notes	Delivered in partnership between RIBA and Oxford Brookes University	Limited take up of Part 1 Apprenticeship by practices; Foundation could shift this. Currently only at London South Bank University)	Note that ongoing exchange with students indicates limited interest; Data here based on marketing research & BE Built Environment PT programmes	This is still the main route to completion of Part 1
Attributes:				
Geographic location of student	Anywhere in the EEA	UK wide, companies with access to Levy; and Major cities (where large firms have so far joined the scheme)	Living in or near a University	Living in or near a University
Cost	2722/a	No cost to apprentice	Commensurate with role in practice	9,250/a
Prerequisite	Portfolio; Interview	A Levels	varies: approx. 128-136 UCAS points; Portfolio; interview	varies: approx. 128-136 UCAS points; Portfolio; interview
Programme co-requirements	Min 25+ hours of work in practice/week	0.8FTE in practice	varies	None
Independent learning	Yes. Students interpret briefs, choose site locations, follow research interests and choose their mentor and personal tutor	Component of each module and varies by module	Component of each module and varies by module	Students work in groups at first and follow key interest to address studio briefs
Personal Tutor	Yes. Tutor with School of Architecture teaching experience. Regular meetings for all subjects	Supervisors collaborate with office mentor to provide tutorial support	Studio tutor (group size approx. 20)	Studio tutor (group size approx. 20)
Contact time at University /examination	up to 8 days/year	1 day/week for 30 weeks	2 days/week	Full time (3 days/week in semester)
Freedom to shift between practices	YES	NO	N/A	N/A
Duration of study	4 years	4 years	4 years	3 years
Academic workload (outside contact hrs)	20 hrs/week	0.2 equivalent	0.2 equivalent	30hrs/week
Award & Accreditation	RIBA and ARB (Part 1), EU	Architecture BA (Hons) RIBA and ARB (Part 1) subject to prescription	Architecture BA (Hons) ARB (Part 1) may be RIBA depending on Institution	Architecture BA (Hons) ARB (Part 1) may be RIBA depending on Institution
Part 3 (only relevant during or after Part 2)	N/A	N/A	N/A	N/A

TABLE 1: COMPARING PART 2 PROGRAMMES

Routes and Stages of Qualification	RIBA Studio Certificate	Apprenticeship	Part time	Full time
Notes	Delivered in partnership between RIBA and Oxford Brookes University	This data is based on Apprenticeship at Oxford Brookes; note that other universities may have different arrangements. Also offered at De Montfort, London South Bank, Northumbria Universities	Note that ongoing exchange with students indicates limited interest; Data here based on marketing research & BE Built Environment PT programmes	This is still the main route to completion of Part 1
Attributes:				
Geographic location of student	Anywhere within EEA	UK wide, companies with access to Levy; and Major cities (where large firms have so far joined the scheme)	Living near/ in the vicinity of the University	Living in or near the University
Cost	2722/a	No cost to apprentice	Commensurate with role in practice	9,250/a
Prerequisite	Completion of ARB Part 1	Completion of ARB Part 1, minimum grade required	Completion of ARB Part 1, minimum grade required	Completion of Part 1 is Optional; Portfolio; Interview; IELTS 6.5
Programme co-requirements	Min 25+ hours of work in practice/week	0.8FTE position in architectural practice	varies	None
Independent learning	Yes. Students interpret briefs, choose site locations, follow research interests and choose their mentor and personal tutor	Yes. Students have opportunity for brief interpretation and to develop research related to practice interests	Component of each module and varies by module	Component of each module and varies by module
Personal Tutor	Yes. Tutor with School of Architecture teaching experience. Regular meetings covering all subjects	Supervisors collaborate with office mentor to provide tutorial support	Studio tutor (group size approx. 13)	Studio tutor (group size approx. 13)
Contact time at University /examination	up to 8 days/year at design examinations	190-200 hours/year contact plus 8-12 half hour online meetings with teaching staff	2 days/week	Full time (2 days/week in semester)
Freedom to shift between practices	YES	NO	N/A	N/A
Duration of study	3 years	4 years (Part 2&3)	3 years	2 years
Academic workload (outside contact hrs)	15 hrs/week	0.2 equivalent	0.2 equivalent	30hrs/week
Award & Accreditation	RIBA and ARB (Part 2), EU	Architecture MArch (Hons) RIBA and ARB (Part 2) subject to prescription	Architecture MArch (Hons) ARB (Part 2) may be RIBA depending on Institution	BArch or Diploma or MArch ARB (Part 2) may be RIBA depending on Institution
Part 3 (only relevant during or after Part 2)	Collect PEDR hours during Diploma; register for Part 3 during or after Diploma completed	Integrated in the 4 year programme	Collect PEDR hours during study register Part 3 after Part 2 completed	Collect PEDR hours after studies completed and register for Part 3 after Part 2 completed

FULL-TIME

Full-time study commonly takes three years as an undergraduate (Part 1) and two years as a postgraduate (Part 2).

PART-TIME

Part-time study is usually two days a week while working, taking four years for undergraduate (Part 1) and three years for postgraduate (Part 2).

Hannah Vowles, Deputy Head of School at Birmingham City University, comments: 'Our part-time students work in practice four days a week and complete the three-year BA course over four years, and two-year MArch over three years. At BA they very quickly become adept at managing their time, their boss, their family and so on. Many of them use their experience and skills to support increasingly ambitious design propositions.'

APPRENTICESHIP

Some schools have embraced the government's apprenticeship scheme, which involves a day a week at university, career appraisal, interview, case study and design challenge. Apprenticeships are free from tuition fees, but you must work in an architect's office. The benefit is that they combine practical experience in an architect's office with academic tuition and earning a salary, although note that there's currently a wider choice of these at Part 2 level.

Recently the RIBA has worked with a group of 20 British architectural practices to develop apprenticeships, and two apprenticeship routes have been approved:

- study for Part 1 recognition to qualify as an architectural assistant
- study for Part 2 and Part 3 level to qualify as a registered architect.

The programmes are each four years long. The experience of everyday architectural practice, reduced financial stress and a network within the wider construction industry is seen as an accessible route for qualification and job opportunities.

ALTERNATIVE ROUTES

Other schools have developed alternative pathways to qualification, including the London School of Architecture, which currently operates at Part 2 level. This allows you to work in an office, which pays your fees and acts as an educational collaborator with the school.

There are other alternative routes to becoming an undergraduate. A selection of schools offer foundation courses (pre-Part 1), which can be full-time or completed while working in an architect's office. For example,

Oxford Brookes University are developing the RIBA Studio foundation course. Maria Faraone, Director, describes its aims: 'It serves as a preparation course for school leavers and those in career transition who are preparing to enter undergraduate education, en route to becoming a registered architect. The Foundation in Architecture is a part-time independent study course with contact time spread throughout the year, comprising seven days in total. Students on the course are expected to be in employment in a practice where their early architectural development will be fostered and financially supported; we will help develop these partnerships.'

Successful completion of the RIBA Studio foundation course facilitates the skills, thinking and passion to prepare students for the journey to becoming an architect. Achievement of Merit will award entry to the RIBA Studio Certificate course (Part 1), where students can remain in practice and continue their blended learning.

Other architecture schools offer degree courses with Part 1 recognition that are four years' duration and incorporate a foundation year. For example, the University of Brighton offers Architecture BA(Hons) with integrated foundation.

Most architecture schools have systems for Accreditation of Prior Experiential Learning (APEL). APEL is the process where credit is sought for learning that has not previously been assessed and awarded credit by an academic institution or professional organisation. Such skills, knowledge and abilities can sometimes be equal to those gained by students following more structured university courses, and it can exempt you from some modules of study or even whole years. It should be acknowledged that this is rare, though, as generally architectural education is highly legislated and prescriptive.

If you feel you have covered the content of a module or modules via your work/life experience, you can make a case with evidence that you have already expertise in these learning outcomes. In architectural education, this is most likely to take the form of extensive years in an architect's office. If this is the case for you, you should talk to individual schools about your experience and whether there is any opportunity for APEL.

Every four to five years, architecture schools are visited by panels of architects from practice and academia, including a student from another institution, for a couple of days. The architects talk to school management, staff and students about a school's direction, ambitions, staffing levels, facilities and ability to meet the Architects Registration Board (ARB) criteria for each part of the process of becoming an architect. They also look at complete portfolios of the design and written work of the students, and the whole process is supervised and coordinated by the RIBA. A report is written and published publicly online, which is how schools are validated or subject to conditions that must be rectified, or commendations for good

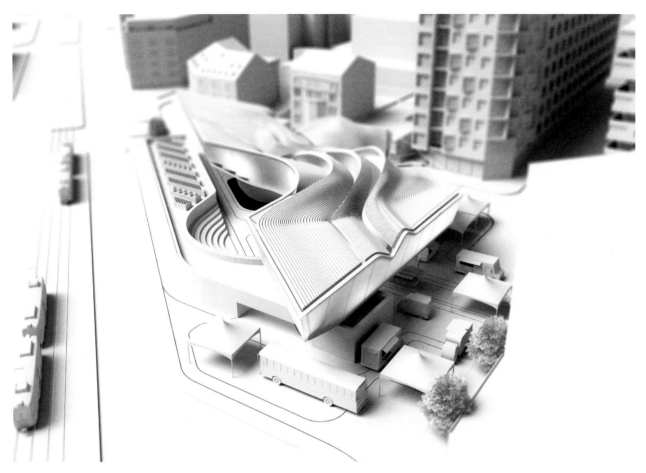

1.7
University of East London, digital printed model by Andreas Stadlmayr, Year 4. **Presentation models for projects can be made in an analogue fashion, or using digital 3D printing, or a mixture of both.**

practice. This document then becomes the basis for a school to apply to the ARB for its proscription as a validated school. Some schools are new, and have what is called 'candidate' status. This means they are in the process of applying for proscription and seek to be validated in due course. If you apply to such a school, you should be fully aware of the school's progress in this process and the timescale involved to understand what status your future qualification will have.

Please see the appendix for additional sources of information on pre-application and applying to schools.

Selecting and applying to schools of architecture

Taking the steps outlined in the previous section to research and understand your options should help you make an informed decision about the schools that are right for you. The next step is to make a final selection of schools and send off your application.

As noted, some schools are more artistic while others are more technically oriented or more politically and socially engaged. It's valuable to

17

understand the genealogy and anatomy of the universities you apply to by researching online. The faculties and facilities at different architecture schools can vary enormously. You'll find that some schools were born out of old art schools that have been assimilated into a university, while others have a historically academic grounding.

First year can be constituted in different ways, with different staff numbers, class sizes and approaches to design studio. Some schools have large first-year intakes, in excess of a hundred students, while others are a little smaller. The size of first year affects the ambiance and teaching methodologies you will experience. Reflect on your own preference and how it could affect your participation.

WHERE TO STUDY?

An important factor is where you want to study – a capital city, a campus university, or somewhere relatively rural with quick access to the countryside. Consider whether you see yourself living at home, or in a hall of residence, or sharing a student house.

London universities benefit from easy access to some of the world's greatest cultural assets: museums, galleries, concert halls, exhibition venues and architectural landmarks. It is a magnet for practising architects, which means academics and visiting practitioners are more varied and easier to find. The downsides are that the costs of accommodation and living costs are high, halls of residence might be relatively far away from the university buildings, and the size and intensity of the city can be overwhelming for some.

A provincial campus university, a short distance from the centre of a city, often in a more rural situation, facilitates a much more student-focused community and perhaps a more hermetic environment in which to study. The positives are that there's typically a greater sense of community with a more closely connected peer group, and most are situated at a shorter distance from the countryside or coast. The downsides are that you're not usually as close to a wide range of cultural experiences (although this depends on the university), and you can feel as though you exist in a university bubble.

Another possibility is a larger city outside of the UK capital, such as Liverpool, Edinburgh or Cardiff, which are all great cities with a long history and famous institutions, where one can benefit from the culture of the city and its distinctive architecture. These typically have a lower cost of accommodation than the UK capital and better national and international transport links than more remote campuses.

In short, each university type offers something different and should be considered carefully.

1.8
University of Coventry,
Community Arts Centre,
Oliver Flew, Year 2.
A section is useful to show elements of a building such as its internal vertical arrangement and the construction of its floors and ceilings, as well as how it meets the ground and the sky.

APPLICATION PROCESS

Most schools of architecture receive applications through UCAS, a centralised online system that notifies the universities you apply to and coordinates the application and acceptance process. (Note that the Architectural Association in London is a private school and must be applied to directly.)

The UCAS form gathers your personal details, qualifications to date and current courses at the point of application. Your current school or sixth form college will anticipate your grades based on performance and will also write a statement about you. The form includes the facility for you to apply to five universities and submit a personal statement. The personal statement gives you the opportunity to explain your skills, passions and reasons for applying to an architecture school. This is important in helping the school to understand you as a person and your motivations for applying.

Things to consider including are your ambitions, your ways of engaging with the world, and your interest in cities and architecture. It's the perfect place to explain your architectural interests, the books on architecture you have read and the contact you've had with architects and schools in an upbeat way. It's useful to have your draft proofread by someone else, to check for spelling, punctuation and grammar. It is a combination of your statement, academic achievements and home institution's statement that will ultimately determine whether you are offered a place or an interview.

Preparing for interview: making a portfolio

Universities can offer places simply by assessing the UCAS form, or they may offer an interview. Many schools of architecture do not accept students without interview, and they spend a lot of time on the interview process. This is to familiarise the prospective student with the school as well as to conduct a dialogue with them about their work.

Taster days are offered by some universities to reveal the experience of academic life. Participating in these activities will help a student make informed choices about which school to attend later. Victoria Farrow, course leader for BA Architecture at Birmingham School of Architecture and Design, explains: 'This gives new applicants a chance to try out our studios, work with staff and produce work for a mini project, and experience what the course is like. It also gives new students the opportunity to chat informally with staff and meet new friends. Students may bring a portfolio along for guidance. We look for individuals with design ambition, a hunger to learn new things and an aspiration to develop and become part of the wider profession.'

Universities may set a task or series of tasks for you before an interview, for you to illustrate your fledgling architectural thoughts and to provide something specifically architectural for you to talk about. You will also be expected to have a portfolio of creative pieces to talk about, which are normally artworks but not always. Anna Gidman from Liverpool University School of Architecture offers insight and advice into the portfolio process: 'There is little architecture shown. The good ones use a variety of media which must be a requirement of A Level art. Generally, when architecture is included, it appears to be drawn from a photograph rather than from life, which is a shame. The filtering is different on location to sitting comfortably at home. Students should get out more and look up.'

A portfolio might not only include artwork. People have been accepted on to courses for writing great poetry, making clothes, pottery, composing music, creating sculptures, or all of the above and more. The portfolio is there to illustrate your creativity over the previous few years and should show you in your best light.

When assembling your portfolio, it's advisable to edit it to show your best work and resist overfilling it with everything you've done. It might

1.9
Birmingham City University,
Architectural Synergies, Will Haynes,
Year 1, MArch.
This computer-generated visualisation illustrates the realism that can be achieved using digital techniques. A synergy of the hand, the eye and the virtual is what every architect should aspire to.

1.10
Bartlett, University College London,
end-of-year show.
One of the most exuberant summer
shows is the Bartlett's. It is always
packed with drawings and models as
units compete for the best display to
illustrate their preoccupations and
student work.

be helpful to get someone else's view on which of your work to include – an art teacher, an artistic family member or a visually aware friend. Furthermore, the make-up of your portfolio may need to change for different schools depending on their focus. If a school has a more technical bias, consider taking out some of the artwork and inserting some design drawings for a product, or similar.

A good portfolio will be portable and not too heavy (A1 is a good size, with approximately 25 sheets). Many prospective students will turn up for interview having carried a heavy portfolio across the country and feel exhausted on arrival.

An interview with a portfolio is likely to be 20 to 30 minutes long. When selecting your work, consider the time and ensure it can be seen by the interviewer and explained in 10 to 15 minutes, allowing time for further discussion and questions. Certain schools may ask you to submit the portfolio in advance, which means you will not be there to explain it and the work will require more captioning. The words you use in portfolios should be direct and minimal: enough to get the message across without over-explanation.

1.11
University of Greenwich, Simona Moneva,
Remnants of War – UXO Risk Assessment
Headquarters, Year 3.
**A large-scale image that attempts to
represent different aspects and views
of the building in one heroic
hand drawing.**

The interview itself

Ensure you arrive early for your interview with time to compose yourself, and dress appropriately for the occasion – usually smart casual. Schools often offer a tour of their facilities by staff or students, and show successful undergraduate portfolios.

Interviews will be conducted either individually or in small groups. Typically, you will be invited to show your portfolio after the interviewer (or interviewers) has introduced themselves. Be explicit about what you tried to achieve with each piece and keep moving through the portfolio. A good tip is to include a strong piece at the beginning and end. This allows you to open by impressing the interviewer and finish with some of your best work remaining visible while the conversation progresses.

Try to be positive and receptive to questions, answering them directly and succinctly. Be self-reflective about your work, considering both its strengths and weaknesses. Interviewers will also appreciate it if you reiterate the research you undertook to choose their particular school as one of your five, expanding on the points made in your personal statement. You will likely be asked who your favourite architects are, so try to learn how to pronounce their names, and know their key buildings, why their work is like it is and why you like it.

Prepare a list of between five and seven questions to ask at the end of the interview. These might include questions about the student experience: where do the school's students come from, how are the courses are taught, or how many students stay on for Part 2? What types of practices do students work in after their degree? When will I know the result of the interview? These questions will both demonstrate a willingness to learn on your part and provide you with insight into the school experience.

If you are lucky, you could be made an offer at the end of the interview, but don't be distressed if this doesn't happen. Each school is different in this respect, and it's best to resist asking how you did. Often the interviewer(s) will want to consider your application in relation to others.

Frosso Pimenides, Director of First Year at University College London's Bartlett School of Architecture, says she looks for the following in a prospective first-year applicant: 'Any hand skills to express and communicate their ideas, mind, soul, curiosities and their personality are important. Any possibility for a conversation: a dialogue when both parties can listen to each other (and not a prepared, endless and tedious speech or instructed performance). Also adaptability, humour, readiness, improvisation and enthusiasm to learn.'

1.12
Bartlett, University College London, workshop.
Schools of architecture should have access to digital and analogue modelling and fabrication workshops, and technicians who can help students realise their projects in model or built form.

Offers, results and clearing

The five universities you have chosen will in most cases make conditional offers based on their standard architectural UCAS tariffs, which vary between institutions. However, Cambridge and other Russell Group research-intensive universities often have the highest tariffs. These tariffs are the points that your GCSE and A Level grades add up to. These then translate back to the A Level grades you must attain to be finally enrolled as a student at a given university. Some universities can reduce your tariff by one A Level grade if you decide to put them as first choice, and you will also be expected to notify UCAS of an 'insurance' offer.

1.13
University of Greenwich, Paride Saraceni, Performative Sonitectures, Barcelona, Year 2 MArch.
Digital techniques can illustrate atmospheric ambiences, often more effectively than hand drawing. The design of architectural augmented space and atmospheres is becoming a preoccupation of some architects.

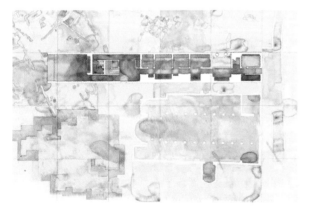

1.14
Edinburgh of University, Alex Abadjieva, Library of Cartography, Year 2.
A subtle and beautifully crafted, delicate plan of a simple building – shown in its context. The way the project is presented reflects its programme and function.

How you decide which two offers to accept is often a complex mix of tactics and emotions. All the research on which five schools to pick comes in handy at this point. Pick the primary one that lives up to your expectations, situation and how you see yourself studying for the next three years or longer, and pick the second one as your back-up.

1.15
Royal College of Art, London,
Live Project at Manifesta12,
Year 4 master's.
Students often work in groups to produce architectural interventions in the city. These can take the form of interior pieces or larger exterior pieces that exhibit architecture or performances.

If you have no offers, you can reapply the following year and in the meantime consider evening classes to improve your portfolio or knowledge of matters architectural.

You might also consider alternative routes into the profession or different built environment professions such as project management, quantity surveying, planning or real estate, or decide to follow other creative pursuits such as interior architecture, graphic design, illustration, fine art, sculpture, carpentry, game design or many more.

If you already have qualifications that add up to a University's tariff, you might be offered an unconditional offer, which means you have been accepted on to the course (and you can choose to accept or reject the offer). This may also be the case if you haven't received your qualifications yet but interviewed well, or if you have prior architectural learning and experience and they wish to accept you on that basis.

After your exams are completed, it's always helpful to read more books on architecture. Look at the way different architects sketch, and read about the history and theory of architecture. Try to imagine and understand what real architects do, the priorities they have and the reasons behind their work and designs. These are different for every architect and every context.

If you've received your results and attained the grades you need for either of your choices, take the time to celebrate!

STUDENT LOANS

You can apply for a student loan without yet having secured a place at a school of architecture. If you need a loan, apply as early as possible for peace of mind. It can be daunting taking out a loan of this magnitude and, if you are approved, it's important to budget sensibly for each term. Architectural courses can be expensive, which means it's important to take the costs of equipment and materials into account. See the appendix for more information on applying for a student loan.

If you haven't met your grades, you will go into clearing. Universities can lower their tariffs at this point and open unfilled places on their courses to those who didn't initially apply to their school. Typically, the schools set aside thousands of phone lines for this purpose, so do phone those that interest you. Most clearing activity happens in the first two days after results, which means it's important to start calling early and keep in mind that you don't have to stick to the universities that you originally applied for. This is where your original research on schools becomes important again and helps you decide who to call.

1.16
University of East London, open studio event.
Frequently architecture schools have visiting critics, lecturers and workshops. These types of events open the students' minds to other ideas sometimes not represented within the school itself.

Once you've been accepted, your course information and reading list should be made available shortly afterwards. Take the time to look at the key primary reading over the summer, and familiarise yourself with your timetable. Get equipment lists, which tend to include drawing instruments, materials and advice on laptops and their computing capacity for the digital architectural graphics and modelling you will be taught. Secondhand bookshops often have great architecture books, while some schools have tables of free books and other equipment deposited for reuse by tutors and students. You might also be able to buy materials and instruments from previous students online or in person at a reduced rate. Computer software will be supplied on the school's machines, and some schools loan out laptops.

Having made a number of academic, financial and practical decisions to reach this point, you are now ready to enter architectural education. Being an architectural student involves ambition, steadfastness and, most importantly, much enjoyment. The next chapter will introduce you to this fascinating, rewarding world.

Five ways to get ahead

1. Find out what an architect does on a day-to-day basis.
2. Try to undertake at least a little work experience in an architect's office.
3. Understand the various routes to achieving Part 1 and decide which route is appropriate for you and your finances.
4. Research appropriate architecture schools through open days, taster days, websites and social media.
5. Apply early, develop an effective personal statement and think about your portfolio. (Some universities don't interview; you will not need a portfolio in this case.)

First Year

This chapter will guide you through some of the different events you are likely to face when you first join a school of architecture. It discusses the initial year of study and offers advice on how to deal with the many new experiences that come with an architectural education. It includes guidance on your first tutorial, your first presentation to a critical audience, the initial exercises you may be asked to participate in, the types of drawings you'll be expected to produce and the ways to conceive of architectural space and sites.

Architectural education at undergraduate (RIBA Part1) level and postgraduate (RIBA Part 2) level is predicated on the following 11 criteria, and your education as an architect will be measured against them. At undergraduate level, by the end of Part 1, you will be expected to have a broad knowledge of these subjects. At postgraduate level, by the end of Part 2, you will also be expected to demonstrate considerable and complex critical knowledge and dexterity. The criteria are as follows:

1. Understanding architectural design and its aesthetic and technical requirements.
2. Knowledge of history and theory of architecture and related arts, technical and human science subjects.
3. Knowledge of the fine arts and their influence on architectural designs.
4. Knowledge of urban design, planning and skills in planning processes.
5. Understanding the relationships between people and their built environment.
6. Understanding the profession of architecture and the role of the architect in society, preparing briefs and taking account of social factors.
7. Understanding methods of investigation for the preparation of architectural building briefs.
8. Understanding structural, constructional and engineering problems to be solved in buildings.
9. Understanding physical problems of climate control, environmental comfort and protection.
10. How to meet building users' requirements for cost management and complying with building regulations.
11. Knowledge of the construction industries organisations, regulations and processes required to translate conceptual designs into actual buildings.

2.1
University College London,
Mabel McCabe, 'Vertical Launderette,
a Rejection of the Modern Washing
Machine', Year 1 BSc.
The ability to envision three
dimensional space and form is a
fundamental skill of the architect.
First year, wherever it is, is formed
around getting the student to
understand this and be able to
represent and model this three
dimensionality swiftly.

Before you've even arrived at university, social media can help you form friendships and support networks. It enables different cohorts of students to chat, with future coursemates, as well as people joining the same school, to discuss a variety of architectural, academic, pastoral and social topics.

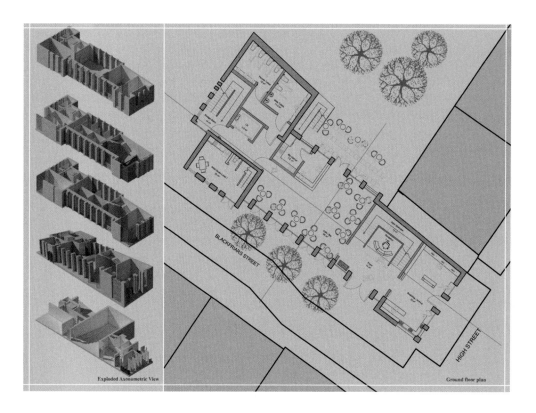

Exploded Axonometric View

Ground floor plan

Facing Elevation of Blackfriars street

2.2, 2.3
University of Strathclyde, Laura Krumina, Gallery in the City 1 + 2, Year 1.
This suite of drawings show the project in a simple way, including plan, key elevation and how it fits into its context, the internal configurations and the building materiality.

The fundamentals

2.4
London South Bank University,
Ellie Spencer, Spatial Intervention,
Year 1.
Here, this first-year student is experimenting with creating spaces within other architectural space and using its performative nature.

The first day as a functioning architectural student is a big step, and the first time you will meet your year group. Most of these people will be your peer group right through your degree and probably beyond, and it will also be the first time you meet most of your tutors for the year. Be attentive to what the tutors have to say, read any course documentation you are given, and read through the course handbook, which will contain a wealth of valuable information about both the course and the university.

It is common practice for students to be allocated a pastoral care tutor. Pastoral or personal tutors are there so that you can talk to someone who is not involved with your academic work about more personal matters, if you need to.

2.5
Birmingham City University,
Diana Grigorie, Architectural
Landscaping, Warley Woods, Year 1.
This presentation model illustrates the student's desire to try to dissolve the distinction between the outside (landscape) and the inside (building) in the project.

UNIT SYSTEM VS YEAR SYSTEM

The structure of your first year is dependent on the university and will be explained by your tutor. Schools work on one of two systems: the 'year' system or the 'unit' system.

- The 'year' system means you will mostly work on the same problem and site collectively to produce a design, aided by a selection of tutors (either full-time or visiting weekly).
- The 'unit' system encourages a bit of competition between units. A unit normally has two tutors, who work with a small number of students. The optimum size for a unit is 15 students, although it can function with up to 20 students. A unit usually has a unique selling point to do with the preoccupations of the tutors, following a given brief or students developing their own brief.

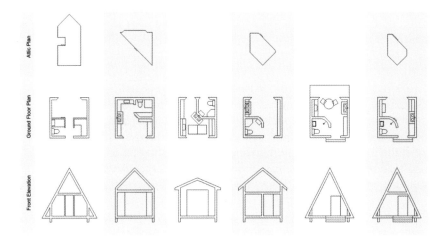

2.6
University of Coventry, George Wade, Chouse, Year 1.
This short drawn project is an exercise in the taxonomy of a small domestic space and its variations; its three-dimensional form changes, likewise where it is cut in plan.

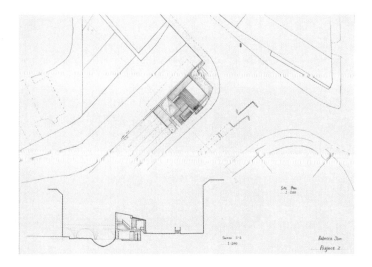

2.7
University of Edinburgh, Rebecca Sun, Assembly, Year 1.
This delicately drawn site plan shows the student's building in context and how it relates to roads and the buildings around it.

BRIEFS

In practice, a brief in its simplest form is the instructions from a client with a list of requirements and directions for the architect to meet. It typically specifies a site, the size and type of building, whether it's a permanent or transient piece of architecture, and whether it's in a public or private space. It may also include a 'schedule of accommodation', which is a list of all the facilities/rooms required, and their sizes.

One of the first tasks an architect must undertake is helping the client develop a clear brief and schedule of accommodation, understanding the interrelationships between facilities and their environmental and structural needs. It will also typically include the client's budget for the project.

In architecture school, briefs are commonly less detailed and more poetic, allowing for student interpretation and creativity. As a first year, briefs will be relatively simple at the beginning to familiarise students with the process. Often the first briefs will be done in groups to encourage teamwork and bonding.

STUDIO

One of the important aspects of architecture school is the development of what is called 'studio culture' and camaraderie between students. In architectural education much is learned on a peer-to-peer basis. Students help each other understand concepts, develop skills and discuss each other's work in a mutually supportive way. This is at its most effective when they are working together on projects in the studio.

There is a view that the continued adherence to studio teaching is somehow parochial, and not reflective of how modern architectural knowledge is gathered. However, there's a counter-argument that there is still value to a process of close, iterative, personalised teaching, and that the supportive structure of the studio with peer learning is worthwhile to teach the diversity of skills and technological expertise required by contemporary architects.

Frosso Pimenides elaborates on studio culture: 'You create a studio culture where sometimes the needs and nature of projects force students to work together and have fun together. Learning to debate, to accept differences of opinion, is often a huge challenge. Extra-mural, often irrelevant events – like a trip, meal, gig, film screening, or protest – enable natural bindings, which is better than forced, socially conventional coexistence.'

Speaking on life-long relationships, Thomas Bryans of the IF_DO architectural practice recalls how he met his two business partners at architecture school: 'If you were to tell our 18-year-old selves that we would eventually set up a practice together, we'd probably be delighted!

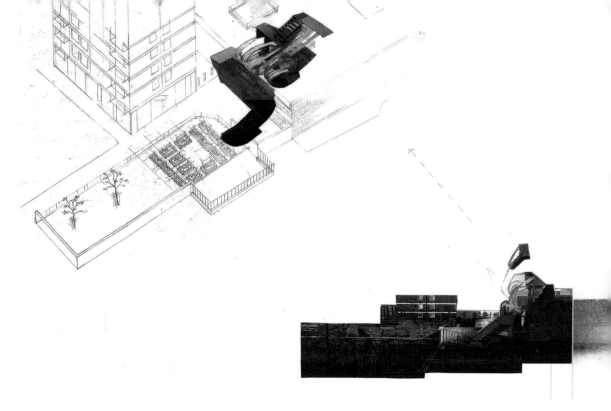

2.8
University of East London,
Eugene Yu Jin Soh, Year 1.
Multiple views of an urban insertion that simultaneously explores light, views, interior and exterior spaces and their materiality.

The three of us met on our first day, and the first four years of our training was shared, learning from the same teachers, and working on the same projects. Having that common starting point is fundamental to the way we work today.' This shows the potential value of relationships formed even on your first day when working together.

You will probably be divided into small groups, and these groups might be reconstituted for each task so that you get to work with a wider selection of students. The tasks will illustrate some basic concepts of architecture.

STRUCTURE

The following example shows a UK university first-year project structure and the relationship between students and tutors:

- First-year students work on six projects during the year (two group projects and four individual projects).
- For each project, students work in small studio groups alongside a dedicated tutor. Each week the student groups meet their studio tutor to discuss and explore their design responses and receive feedback.
- After each project, the students are assigned to a new student group and a new tutor.

The chance to work with different students and tutors helps to build confidence and flexibility in approaches, as well as adjusting to a diverse set of opinions and feedback.

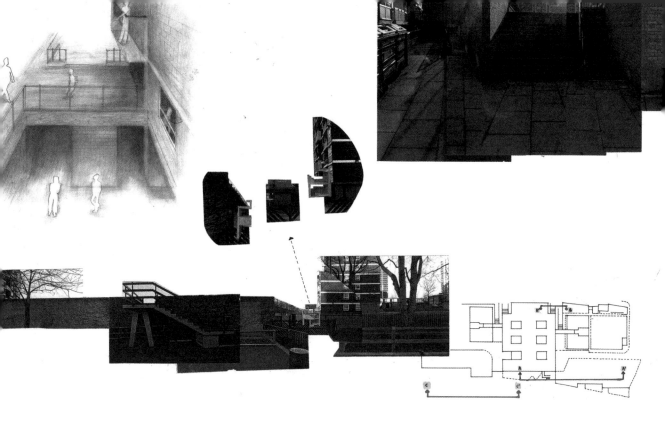

Key concepts you will learn during the first year are how to prioritise, the difference between mass and architectural space, and why architects make drawings, among others.

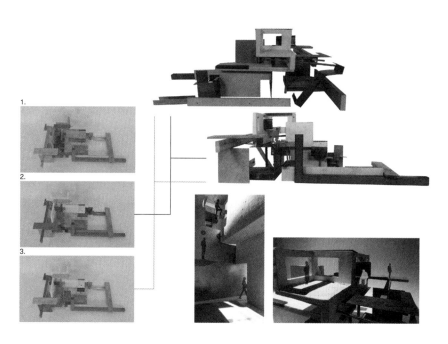

1.

2.

3.

2.9
University of East London, Kalin Petrov, working sketch model, Year 1.
The multiple photographs show how the student is using the model and its reconfiguration to speculate about possible spatial architectural effects on users.

TASKS

When starting at school, you will be given various tasks to help you understand the fundamentals of architecture and working as a team. The following examples offer a glimpse into the sorts of projects you might undertake during your first year.

TASK EXAMPLE 1:

To emphasise the importance of prioritising and thinking around a problem, the students are stranded on the Moon and have an hour to make a camp for survival with a series of domestic implements (string, spoons, knives), gaffer tape, a rubber dinghy, a blanket and some sticks.

Note: Of course the task is impossible, as the gravity is a sixth of what it is on Earth, but this hypothetical situation enables groups to discuss the condition of their 'site', the materials of their given items and proposed ways to assemble them. Another common task along these lines is to construct you own workspace within the studio from a set of given materials, which involves negotiation and attention to how materials might go together.

TASK EXAMPLE 2:

The students must make a sculpture with a standard builder's concrete block, illustrating the notion of creating void from mass and then sketching it.

Note: Conducted over a few days, this task is designed to show that architectural space can be made from removing matter as well as adding it.

TASK EXAMPLE 3:

Small groups of students are given children's building blocks and some cardboard insides of kitchen rolls and a gridded baseboard, with the lines numbered up one side and lettered across the bottom. Each team, in a separate room, must make a construction. Then they must communicate its design in a specific way to another team to enable them to mimic the first team's design without seeing it. The modes of communication are phone call, prose writing and drawing.

2.10
University of Dundee, Immanuel Lavery,
Casting, Year 1.
**A similar exercise as Task 2, the casting
of objects provokes an understanding
of positive and negative space (mass
and void) and the role they can play in
the making of architecture.**

Note: The phone call and the prose instructions will probably fail to
produce an accurate likeness in the other team's construction. However,
the drawn instructions tend to be a reasonable success, and could be
located on a baseboard by a series of coordinates.

Ultimately, this is why architects draw – to communicate ideas and to
accurately place materials relative to one another.

SPACE

All these tasks promote teamwork, bonding, imagination, creativity,
negotiation and clear explanation to other parties, which are key to
any architect's work. Whichever way your school gets you to see these
principles, they are crucially important to understand, and illustrate ways
of making 'space'.

Why do architects talk about space and not rooms? Architects see the
world as a series of spaces that flow into one another. The notion of
'rooms' is almost too prescriptive. Rooms imply defined areas with doors,
floors and ceiling, but these are merely one type of space – a cellular
space. A park is a space with other spaces within it formed by buildings,
trees, ponds and hedges, for example. Objects mould and define scales
of space, and space is fluid. Whatever happens on your first day of
architecture school, it will revolve around notions of architectural space.

39

First-term drawing, modelling and scaling

DRAWING

The value of drawing to represent your architectural thoughts is paramount. At the start of your architectural student career, you will be asked to draw spatial and material ideas.

Hannah Vowles discusses an architect's ability to sketch and draw in these terms: 'Drawing and sketching, including sketch models, are key to communication, first of all with yourself, externalising ideas, testing them through trial and error; and then with co-designers, colleagues, clients, students and users. The speed, contingency, variation and disposability of the sketch is crucial. Students need to learn not to be too precious about sketches, and to see them as iterative means to possible ends.'

The sketch is an initial, vital part of the design process. A sketch is important for putting ideas on paper, but is also open to misinterpretation, thereby actively contributing to the design process. You might ask how? A 'hairy' sketch can represent various materials, alignments and junctions simultaneously, and therefore can produce ill-conceived alternate solutions to a problem or spatial arrangement. As you become more experienced, you will be able to quickly use sketching and its revelatory aspects to identify issues and further your design thoughts.

While contemporary practice predominantly uses digital tools to produce work (which is covered later), the modern architect should be proficient in both traditional analogue techniques and digital techniques. Mark Garcia, Senior Lecturer at Greenwich University, remarks that 'it is not a binary "versus" but a question of "both/and"'.

At the beginning of your student career, it is important to manually work up ideas. There are many advantages to the digital ways of doing things; however, one of the disadvantages is that computers do not allow you to viscerally experience or feel your work through the movement of your body while making it. These haptic sensations make you familiar with the geometries of the component parts of your designs. Being unable to draw in the traditional sense can lead to sanitised, overly complex work predicated on particular software. As time goes on, you will also learn to sketch at scale.

SCALE

What is scale? To start with, note that there is no such thing as 'free scale'. Scale is a proportionalised system that allows large structures to be drawn in proportion, accurately but small enough to be transcribed on reasonable sizes of paper, which is done using a scale rule.

PLANS

What is a plan? Architects represent their ideas and designs in combinations of a wide variety of views. Some representations are two-dimensional (plan, section, elevation), others three-dimensional (isometric, axonometric, perspective) and some four-dimensional (utilising film and animation).

Plans are aerial views or horizontal cuts or sections through buildings, so smaller-scale plans (1:1250, 1:2500, etc.) can show the position of a site on a map, its orientation relative to the points of the compass, your project and how it fits into its surroundings – effectively, its urban context. At a larger scale (1:100, 1:50) the layout of the spaces within a building can be shown, and at an even larger scale (1:20, 1:5, 1:1) details emerge.

When you draw a plan, it is convention to black in the parts of the building you have cut through to draw the plan. A section is the same, but a vertical cut through a building that reveals floors stacked above one another and the make-up of floorplates; again the convention is to black in elements you have cut through. Section lines are marked

2.12
Bartlett, University College London,
Bartlett Studio.
This studio image shows a student carefully making a scale model.

41

on the corresponding plan to show where the cut has been taken and the direction of view. Elevations are flat-on drawings of the outside walls, or in some cases the inside walls, of buildings and objects. See the appendix at the back of this book for reference sources that will teach you the protocols of architectural drawing.

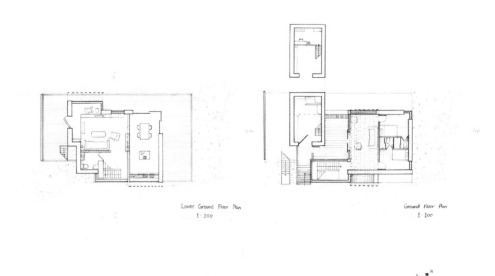

Lower Ground Floor Plan
1 : 100

Ground Floor Plan
1 : 100

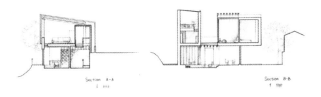

Section A-A
1 : 100

Section B-B
1 : 100

Rebecca Sun
Project 2

North-West Elevation
1 : 100

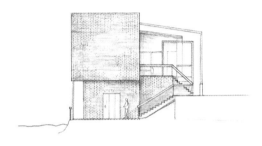

South-west Elevation
1 : 100

AXONOMETRIC, ISOMETRIC AND PERSPECTIVE DRAWING

A crucial element in your architectural tool kit will be your ability to draw and represent your ideas in three dimensions. To do this you will need to learn how to use the axonometric, isometric and perspective projections, as the ways to make a two-dimensional drawing appear three-dimensional. Axonometric and Isometric drawings can be created by taking a plan or section of an object or building, setting it to an oblique angle and projecting vertically up or down the actual dimension of walls and windows. Perspective drawings are different and rely on the lines of your drawing of your building/object converging on `vanishing points' to give the illusion of distance. There are numerous ways to construct a perspective, they can have one, two or multiple vanishing points. There are references on how to develop these types of drawings in the appendix.

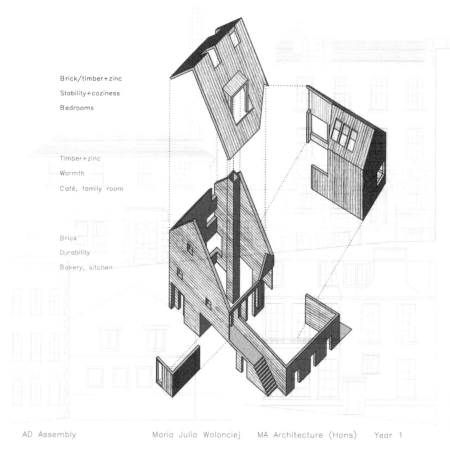

Brick/timber+zinc
Stability+coziness
Bedrooms

Timber+zinc
Warmth
Café, family room

Brick
Durability
Bakery, kitchen

AD Assembly   Maria Julia Wolonciej   MA Architecture (Hons)   Year 1

Material Follows Function[1]

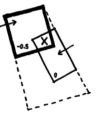

Celebrating conflict between site geometries through brick and timber in zinc envelope, with a chimney at their intersection

Neighbouring brick tower reference

Baker's house, New Town, Edinburgh

Axonometric, 1:250, background façades: A.Brown

[1] Paraphrasing Sullivan's 'Form (ever) follows function'

MODELLING

Analogue modelling is important in starting to understand structure. If you can model it in the real world, it's likely to stand up when built. This is not always true when designing virtual models, and it is a crucial distinction between the two types of modelling. Alongside analogue techniques, however, you should familiarise yourself with a few digital tools such as Photoshop. Photoshop is an advanced collaging and image editing software, and your school will probably have a licence for it, with tutorial software.

Some parts of your designs will have moving parts, which means you will need to know how to represent their loci and trajectories. Use of dotted lines is the standard; however there are many other ways such as film, digital projection and animation. While you may not yet have expertise in these, it is valuable to acquire some of these skills too. Considering advancements in technology, it's likely that the future of architecture will be at the boundary of the virtual and the actual. Depicting motion and engineering will be crucial.

2.16
University of Edinburgh, Maria Wolonciej, Strangely Familiar Assembly, Year 1.
This student uses the conventions of an exploded axonometric to illustrate the general arrangement of her building.

The first building brief: becoming a proper architect

A some point you will be given a brief that's about designing a simple building and you will start to feel like a proper architect. The brief will probably have a schedule of accommodation and a site.

EXAMPLE BRIEF:

A small photographer's studio, living space and gallery.

SITE ANALYSIS

The first step is to go to your site and conduct an analysis, which will include the following:

- Reviewing site photographs
- Finding different scale maps of the area
- Assessing the site history
- Understanding the proximity and materiality of the buildings around and their rights of light
- Possible ways to access the site – both existing and potential
- Understanding the site's orientation relative to the points of the compass
- Recording the heights of the surrounding buildings and their shapes (their form and massing)
- Understanding and recording views of the site down roads and pathways, as well as (ideally) adjacent buildings
- Understanding what will be under your building – soil structure, tube lines and power cables, for example – and whether it's susceptible to flooding

Out of these conditions comes the context of your building.

Look at precedents. There will be many examples of galleries and photographic studios which you can visit at roughly the same size as yours, perhaps even in a similar site context. Assess their plans and sections, how they form the dark rooms to avoid light, how they facilitate various light conditions in the studio and how they deal with light in the gallery. Consider the scale of exhibits – how does the gallery facilitate different exhibition layouts, and how does it hang work? How do the public circulate through the public spaces of the building, and how are the more private spaces of the building accessed and separated from the public spaces? Look at the materials that are used: the walls, floor, ceiling finishes. How does the whole thing stand up? What's it like after dark? Talk to professional photographers about what they want.

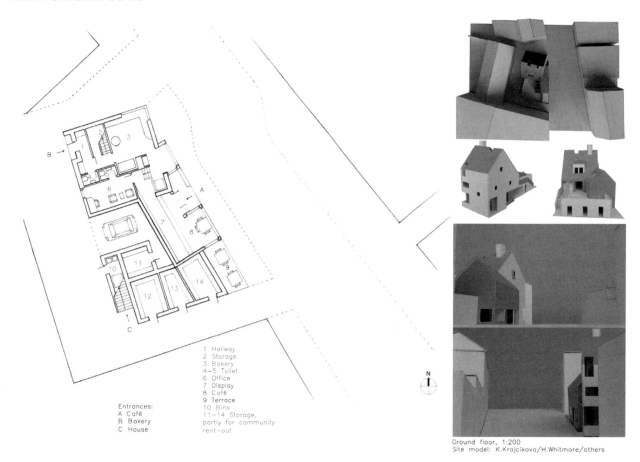

1 Hallway
2 Storage
3 Bakery
4-5 Toilet
6 Office
7 Display
8 Café
9 Terrace
10 Bins
11-14 Storage,
partly for community
rent-out

Entrances:
A Café
B Bakery
C House

Ground floor, 1:200
Site model: K.Krajcikova/H.Whitmore/others

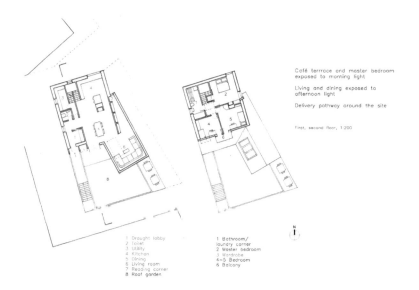

Café terrrace and master bedroom
exposed to morning light

Living and dining exposed to
afternoon light

Delivery pathway around the site

First, second floor, 1:200

1 Draught lobby
2 Toilet
3 Utility
4 Kitchen
5 Dining
6 Living room
7 Reading corner
8 Roof garden

1 Bathroom/
laundry corner
2 Master bedroom
3 Wardrobe
4-5 Bedroom
6 Balcony

2.17, 2.18, 2.19, 2.20
University of Edinburgh, Maria Woloncıej,
Strangely Familiar Assembly, Year 1.
**This project exhibits models, sections,
level plans and perspectives. It is a
good example of a Year 1 project that
describes the architectural aspirations
of the student towards site, context,
space and materiality.**

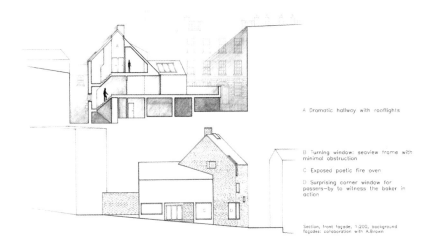

A Dramatic hallway with rooflights

B Turning window: seaview frame with minimal obstruction

C Exposed poetic fire oven

D Surprising corner window for passers—by to witness the baker in action

Section, front façade, 1:200, background façades: collaboration with A.Brown

Seaviews:
master bedroom,
reading corner,
kitchen

Special thanks:
Rachael Scott
Jamie D. Henry

LIGHTING

In terms of lighting, it's crucial to remember that the sun rises in the east and sets in the west and will cast shadows over your site. Furthermore, whatever building you design will also cast shadows over itself and its context. For example, glazing facing north will let in the purest light for painting, and glazing facing south is optimal for solar gain (heat). The latter can be good if handled well and the heat is stored for energy usage, but it can be bad if the room is a primary workspace, because south-facing spaces can be unpleasant to remain in for long periods.

PRIORITISATION AND CONCEPT

Establishing the orientation of your design should be done quickly, otherwise you might be prone to a pitfall known as 'displacement activity'. This is where a student overworks on anything except the design. An example of displacement activity, in this context, might be visiting and analysing the site too many times, producing page upon page of data, plans and sections. Another example would be producing long schedules of photographic equipment and lens types. Displacement activity can make you feel as though you've put in a huge amount of work but without achieving your objective. Therefore, it's essential to establish priorities.

The priority here is understand your brief, the context of your site and the nature of the spaces you will need to design swiftly. The difficult part is not defining the problem, necessarily – it is designing a solution that works on the many levels that you are now familiar with.

It's necessary to understand the interrelationships of different spaces within your building, their environmental conditions (for example, lightness and darkness) and their scales relative to each other. Some might be double-height, while others will be more domestic and single-storey.

Typically, a building needs a guiding 'concept' that helps the architect design it, and this evolves from the type of building and its site. The concept should be communicated by a simple diagram, which might show for example how the building is organised around a structural spine. Alternatively, it could show the relationship of the building's inside to its exterior spaces, or how the building construction methods change relative to the scale of space within – for example, the gallery space might be a lightweight steel structure. Smaller-scaled spaces might be domestic brick and timber construction, which can be diagrammed too.

Be wary of developing a plan, followed by the section, then followed by the elevation. You must work simultaneously in plan, section and elevation, while considering structure, environmental conditions, function and contextual massing, while also considering how the building is made, keeps out bad weather, accepts good weather, mediates the ground plane and meets the sky. This all takes practice, and more often than not many years of experience, and your first attempt will be at the low end of an exponential curve.

As architect Ian Ritchie observes: 'Students [should] cultivate an understanding of architecture's function and of the biological and neurological history that goes into the way buildings and urban development affect us, rather than let themselves be seduced by superficial architectural form-making. A beautiful building is pointless if its systems and human dimensions don't work.'

Try not to be worried if it's a little unsettling to begin with. Architectural education is like going to the gym – you go day after day, and over time your creative muscles become taut and strong, and your exercises will become more complex and demanding. At first, there are bound to be some aches and pains.

MATERIALS

Buildings are made of materials, and there are many different types of materials. Each type of material is manufactured in different ways (think sustainability) and can be joined in different ways. It may respond to water in different ways, and may be best used in buildings in different ways.

Bricks, for example, are strongest when supporting a weight from directly above (they are strong in compression). Meanwhile steel, when detailed correctly, is strongest when things are suspended or pulled upwards by it (it is strong in tension).

In your early designs, you will probably use simple notions of construction and structure – the oldest and most common is a 'trabeated' structure, which is derived from the post and lintel. Imagine two poles, set slightly apart, supporting another pole that spans between them. This spanning piece then becomes a truss, and the vertical poles are columns (primary structure). When you get a series of columns and trusses you can also span between them with smaller structural members (secondary structure). You can span again with even smaller structural members or boards of material (tertiary structure). This common structural system needs to be cross-braced to stop it twisting under load, which is done by bridging diagonally some of the gaps between columns and columns, and trusses and trusses.

At this early stage in your career, it's natural to feel frustration when you don't know some basic structural rules of thumb. In real life, a structural engineer would check and specify all the structural elements of the building in conjunction with the architect's aesthetic and conceptual concerns. Without this structural knowledge, students often under- or over-estimate structural depth and sizes. Look at the sizing of structural members around you, particularly those of buildings that are similar in size to the building you are designing (see the appendix for reference sources for structural concepts and methods).

Another common flaw in first-year student work is the lack of provision of cores or risers and service runs in building designs. Buildings have a variety of routes through which water pipes, flues and electrical and digital cables run from space to space. If vertical, these are called 'risers' or 'cores'; cores often contain lifts. If horizontal they are called 'service runs'. Water needs to be separated from electricity; both need to be accessible.

CONCEPT DIAGRAM

Remember the concept? Your finished design for a building should reflect your concept diagram right through to the materials specified. The concept diagram should be readable at all scales within the final proposal. This will take time and knowledge to achieve, so try to study how successful architects do this. Your concept should also influence the way you draw your final proposal and how you compose a series of presentation images.

Images for your first building proposal

When tackling your first building proposal, you will need to make a list of drawings that will form the core of all future presentations within school, and later as a professional. The images will depend on the project – they may all be drawn by hand, or on the computer, and they will be different projections and at different scales. It is best to assess the strength of each method of production and not prefer one over another at this stage of your course. You must become proficient in both digital and manual methods. While the following list of work is not definitive, it is a useful starting point.

1. **Location plan** – showing where your site and proposition are located within the city or countryside (1:1250 is a good scale for this). Try to orient all plans with north at the top of the image.

2. **Site plan** – showing the building on its site, and how it responds to its neighbours and its primary access routes – this may also show the building roof plan (all scales will be chosen to be commensurate with the scale of the building).

3. **Series of level plans** – starting with the ground floor and working upwards if there is more than one floor. Drawings should show columns and/or load-bearing walls and maybe the dotted lines of primary structure/trusses above.

4. **Two key sections** one lateral and one transverse at the same scale as the plans, with section lines marked on the plans.

5. **Key elevations** – ideally showing neighbouring context.

6. **Structural diagram** an isometric or axonometric projection is good for this.

7. **Series of perspective sketches** – showing how the building reveals itself as you approach it, or as you walk past. As with the elevation, try to represent the materiality of the building.

8. **Series of sketch interiors** – showing how lovely and special the inside of your building could be.

9. **Section from ground to eaves** – (1:20), perhaps with details explored at a larger scale (1:5).

10. **Site model or sketch models** – make sure you record them photographically for future presentation.

You are strongly advised to attend all tutorials as timetabled, and to listen to your tutor, take notes and listen to other students. You should also stay for other students' tutorials, as you will learn from these too. All of the above images should be discussed with your tutors – so it is important that you have a good relationship with them and take their advice. Each school is different, with varying emphasis on what you should learn and in what order, so your tutors will guide you. At the end of the project, a final crit will be timetabled.

The first serious crit: a user's guide

What is a 'crit'? A crit (sometimes called a 'review' or 'jury') is an opportunity for you to present your work/building to your tutors, invited guests and student colleagues in public. A crit is typically 20 to 30 minutes long, and once you've succinctly presented your work, the critics will respond to it and advise on steps moving forward, while highlighting mistakes, further opportunities, further references and other precedents, and discussing the project concept and its appropriateness. Crits are further divided into interim crits and final crits.

Interim crits are 'formative' and happen at various stages as your design progresses to help you focus on the important matters for that stage of the project. For example, one interim crit might address site context and overall building orientation, while another one addresses structure and services. A final crit occurs at the end of a project to sum up what you have done well and point out where improvements might be made in future projects.

Why do we have crits? Well, they are wonderful learning tools and encourage creative dialogue. They give you the opportunity to discuss your ideas in a wider forum and to practice a crucial architectural skill – orally presenting your work, supplemented by images. This skill is crucial to your academic and future professional life, as you will be interviewed for positions in an office, or will need to pitch for commissions or give talks on your work.

Many architectural tutors are keen advocates of crits. Mark Garcia has a creative take on them: 'The review of all architectural research as a live, rhetorical, real-time, action, polemic, event, performance, experiment and oration is essential and can become a form of emergent and conceptual art itself. However, this kind of happening requires commitment, optimism,

2.21
Bartlett, University College
London, Bartlett crits.
Crits are a common rite of passage
for students, and they can be
great teaching tools, providing
insight into what you are trying
to achieve as a student.

manners, ambition, skill, magnanimity, knowledge, diplomacy, altruism, tolerance, humour, sensitivity, patience, compassion and experience from everyone concerned.'

The first rule is turn up on time, then pin up your work and, if you're working purely digitally, ensure your PowerPoint presentation or animation works on your computer/screen. As with tutorials, you will learn from attending your colleagues' crits.

Crits often can often trigger nervousness, but they are also immensely rewarding. To try and eliminate nerves, rehearse your narrative and time it at less than 10 minutes. Be clear and strategic, and get to the architectural proposal quickly without spending too much time talking about research.

Often students put in a sustained spurt of work in the days before a crit, sometimes working through the night (even the night before). For your own mental health, it's best to avoid this approach at all costs, as it will leave you tired, stressed, defensive and unresponsive to criticism. If you work consistently every day – avoiding displacement activity – you will be surprised how much quality work can be produced. Last-minute work is prone to poor outcomes in quality and delivery, such as printing work when everyone needs to use the school printers at the same time.

Make sure the size of the work, whether digital or manual, is at an appropriate scale for being viewed by the critics from a seated position three to four metres away. The opportunity to see your work from a distance is good, as you might not normally have the wall space otherwise. This allows you to judge its impact, your ability to communicate your ideas and assess how it might look in an exhibition.

FIRST YEAR

Present the work in the same order as described in the list of images above, starting with the big site picture and progressing to the detail. If all students are developing individual briefs, quickly describe your own. If you are all working on the same brief, your tutors should have made the guest critics aware of this. Explain the site conditions as you have found them, your concept, and then the general arrangement of the building using plans, sections and elevations. Describe how it sits within the city or on its site, how its context frames views of it, how you enter it and how you might circulate through it as different users, also touching on the ambience of its interiors, structure and materiality. A useful tip is to ask a friend or peer to make notes of the critic's comments, so you don't forget the important points afterwards.

2.22
University of Strathclyde, studio review.
The process of describing a scheme and the choosing of images to illustrate your verbal presentation is a skill that all architects will use frequently in practice.

How to write an essay

Architecture school is not all about drawing – it's about designing. Writing is another important skill that an architect requires, and so you need to learn how to 'design' an essay. Helen Castle, Publishing Director at RIBA and ex-editor of *Architectural Design,* regards essay writing as being about 'constructing logical, persuasive arguments'.

An architect spends a lot of time writing and reading – including letters to clients, specifications, contracts, consultation documents, reports, architect's instructions, essays and social media short copy. Certain architects also edit journals, write books and articles, and deal with all sorts of academic writing, which are all ways of getting your ideas and arguments across to a wide range of people.

PREPARATION AND SUBMISSION REQUIREMENTS

Writing is a key architectural skill and can be descriptive in, for example, technical documents that describe how elements of your design are positioned, made and joined. This type of writing will illustrate your ability to deploy material and won't be preoccupied with creating a philosophical argument. Such a document will also rely specifications, diagrams and architectural drawings, and should be direct and concise.

Another variety of writing that you will be required to be familiar with is the academic essay. Academic essays showcase your ability to develop a cogent argument, expressing ideas, logically marshalling evidence, quotations and precedents in support of an overall premise. Information used in this respect must be gained from creditable and authoritative sources (note that Wikipedia is not considered an authoritative or legitimate source in academia, and much web content is unreliable). Referencing is a vitally important aspect of essay writing and should follow either Harvard or Oxford formatting protocols, depending on your school's preference (some schools may use other referencing styles). The failure to correctly attribute other people's thoughts, ideas and prose can lay you open to accusations of plagiarism, which is a serious offence.

When quoting alternative sources, pick out the key concise point that you wish to highlight and introduce it properly in your own words. Essays should predominantly be written in your voice and consist of your thoughts, using the words of others to support your argument. Academic essays are normally written in the third person, so you should not be using 'I' or 'we' or 'you'. Ensure illustrations are appropriate to the argument being constructed and keyed into the text.

Parallel to your studio work will be a series of lectures on all manner of subjects that are relevant to the discipline of architecture, including history and theory of architecture. In the first year, it can take time to understand the interconnected aspects of theory and design, but these become clearer with time and experience. The theoretical side will open you up to more architectural literature, which is very valuable and gives you the tools to answer essay questions in an original and thoughtful way.

STRUCTURE AND STRATEGY

Once you've received your essay question, the first thing is to make sure you understand what you're being asked – study its anatomy. (Sometimes, you might be able to set your own question.) Some do not ask a simple, direct question, which means it's important to consider all aspects of the statement first, including the nuances that might be missed on first read, and which will help you build an argument.

To plan your essay you could draw a diagram of your key points and map its narrative thrust. This will give you a type of tree diagram, beginning with the essay question at the top and finishing with the conclusion.

EXAMPLE QUESTION:

Discuss the 1988 Museum of Modern Art in New York's *Deconstructivist Architecture* exhibition.

First, research the question: find out what this exhibition was about, and which architects were exhibited. Consider the social, political and philosophical context of their work. For example:

- What were the architects' previous architectural preoccupations, who were the curators and what were their biases?
- What impact did the exhibition have internationally?
- Does it really have a deep connection with a previous architectural and political context?
- What other publications picked up the mantle of Deconstructivism?
- What did these architects do subsequently?

Now you need to design your answer and discussion. You will probably have a word count, which determines how much detail you can include; the structure/depth of a 1,500-word essay will be very different to a 5,000-word essay. To decide the importance of each piece of information, establish strategic priorities for your answer. Consider whether information or argument is primary or secondary. The primary points steer the narrative drive of your essay, while the secondary ones are outliers that add to the texture of the essay. Your essay should be as close to the word limit as possible.

Introduction
Structurally, all essays must begin with an introduction outlining what you are going to say. It should introduce the key points you intend to make

before they're substantiated in the main body of the text. It also provides an opportunity to discuss the context of the subject – in this case, the curators and the imperative that made this exhibition topical at that time.

Main body
The main text is where you develop your main arguments.
Before writing this section, it is useful to separate it into a three-part structure, mapping out the three main points and the three important sub-points for each. You may decide that there are more or fewer than three points depending on the essay question; however, it's a useful starting point for thinking strategically.

Conclusion
This is where you summarise your argument, drawing out key points and how you've explained them. It's also a useful place to pose more incisive polemic points that will make the reader think further

The end of first year

End-of-year shows take a variety of forms – sometimes they are closely curated by staff, while on other occasions students are left to their own devices. Sometimes it's a mixture of both – they are an ideal marketing ploy.

The year always ends with a big final crit (for more on crits, see page 51). Expect to be asked to submit your complete first-year portfolio for examination. Prepare your portfolio in chronological order, starting with initial work at the beginning of term one, and culminating in your most recent work. A useful piece of advice is to avoid using plastic sleeves, as schools tend to have overhead lights, which can create reflections that prevent tutors being able to read the drawings properly.

Examiners look for a trajectory of development – conceptually, technically and spatially. Include sketches and work-up drawings to show your process, but avoid the temptation to include random scribbles that have no relevance to the trajectory of your final projects. Try to be strategic without over-editing your work. As your first-year projects have developed in complexity, consider how you have also developed your architectural understanding and design dexterity. Are you showing this succinctly and directly in your portfolio? Your best work should be your most recent project, so ensure images of that project are last in the portfolio, as they will then be the ones the examiners see as they continue to discuss your portfolio.

Different schools have different timetables for the publishing of marks, and differing methods and timescales for determining outcomes and progression decisions. You may know your result before you embark on constructing your end-of-year show, or you may not.

2.23
London South Bank University,
end-of-year show.

The fundamental rule for end-of-year shows is to **participate.** A student who pins up their drawings at the eleventh hour on screens their colleagues have made and painted is most likely to lose support of the group. When the show opens, enjoy the event and be proud of your work! Take the opportunity to reflect on the work of your peers, and look at the years above too, particularly second year. Look at the building types and scales they have been working at and the conceptual and intellectual level of the best work.

If you find out you have passed, congratulations!

This is the first real step to becoming an architect. There are many more steps to go, but this is a major achievement. It's possible you will have a few bits to tidy up over the summer – an essay to rewrite or a few drawings to complete – so ensure these are done well and with diligence to gain your place in second year.

It's possible to fail on too many things to be allowed to correct them over the summer. In this case, review your interest in architecture and consider if it's really the right path for you. If not, take time to review your

2.24
University of Strathclyde,
end-of-year show.

2.25
Royal College of Art show.

options and, if it is, you can usually retake the year. Participating schools
of architecture offer a mentorship scheme to undergraduate RIBA student
members during the autumn and spring in each academic year. It can be
useful to speak to a mentor or your university career advisor at this stage
to help you make an informed decision on your future. Some schools
have parallel degree courses in 'architectural studies', and these are not
ARB/RIBA validated. However, these pathways provide an opportunity
to specialise in architectural history and less prescriptive designing of
objects which are not necessarily buildings, as well as architectural theory
or architectural journalism. Equally, you might decide to move school and
start over again.

Mental health and managing stress

Being a student in architectural education can be stressful in itself. It is not easy and demands hard work, as well as opening yourself to criticism. It is intellectually and often physically tiring, and you are repeatedly required to generate good ideas. All this is difficult at the best of times, which is why it's important to maintain a healthy approach towards managing stress and balancing your workload.

Melissa Kirkpatrick, MArch Part 2 at Sheffield School of Architecture and ambassador for the Architects Benevolent Society has researched mental wellbeing in architecture. She implores: 'In recent years, mental health concerns among architecture students have been increasingly brought to attention, and these problems are often a product of unhealthy cultures cultivated in architecture schools. As a profession, we must continue to raise awareness and educate students, educators and practitioners in order to continue to make positive progress.'

There are common pitfalls that some students encounter during their first year and adjusting can be stressful. Students must be happy to make mistakes and be aware that often more is learned in the act of making a mistake and putting it right than achieving a goal first time around. Students should try to develop an enquiring and exploring mindset – there are no bespoke recipes for success in architectural education, it is all based on the need to explore and experiment.

For a student, time pressures are ever-present. Architects are often required to work quickly to tight deadlines. In the architectural world, deadlines are everywhere as you will deal with clients, planners, contractors and other consultants, and you tend to find yourself working on your own. Satwinder Samra, Director of Collaborative Practice and a Senior Lecturer at the University of Sheffield School of Architecture, has done much work on architectural student wellbeing, and offers valuable insight and advice: 'In the middle of a project, you don't know the answer, things aren't as smooth as you expected and the drawings are unfinished [but] don't worry. It's not you but a natural part of the design process. Developing ideas can be a bit blurry, edgy and full of uncertainty. Each drawing you make will allow you to spot opportunities and reveal the hidden potential in your work. Don't let ideas just exist in your head, get them out by drawing, modelling and sharing with others. That way you'll feel more relaxed and start to enjoy the process. Always try to find drawings and buildings you like. Don't worry if you're not sure why. Trust your gut feeling. You're allowed to have an opinion, and cultivate and nurture your outlook; all great designers are influenced by others.'

Stress can also be increased by poor time management. Establishing priorities and dealing with them in order can alleviate pressure. Seek to develop consistent work patterns and, once you have completed a day of work, making progress, reward yourself. Schedule on a timetable the tasks you have to achieve with deadline dates. It's key to understand your deadlines and identify any 'pinch points' in advance. Equally, work out how long a task might take and ask your tutor if you're unsure. If you have a difficult task to achieve one day, give yourself an easier task the following day. Satwinder Samra advises that working all hours is unhealthy: 'A 24-hour working culture is predicated by certain schools, which only makes students think they have to work longer hours to produce their best work. This isn't good. I always encourage my students to fully engage in all aspects of their lives. That way they can maintain balance and are less likely to become overwhelmed by always "working" on their projects.'

Architect and Mental Wellbeing Ambassador at Assael Architecture Limited, Ben Channon, who has written a book on architecture and wellbeing, comments: 'There's a real temptation in architecture to feel you're too busy to join a sports team, go to the gym, or do other forms of exercise. However, these activities not only help to reduce stress, they have been shown to make you more productive, creative, and better at retaining information when you sit back down to work. Other ways to reduce stress include "mindful" activities such as meditation or yoga. These need not require long periods of time away from your work, which means you can use them even as deadlines approach. Good apps include Headspace, Calm and Five to Nine, which was created by a landscape architect and mindfulness expert.'

Contrary to popular belief, teamwork can be stressful. If you are a talented, ambitious student, being in a mediocre team can be upsetting, particularly if it is detrimental to your grades or the team has not mastered time management. Ben Channon urges you to 'remember that everybody works in different ways and at different speeds, so try your best not to directly compare yourself with others; instead view it as a positive way to learn from others and generate new ideas'.

Failing a year or being asked to repeat over the summer can certainly be difficult, especially if you don't quite understand why. If this is the case, ask your tutors to explain things to you in clear terms so you can work to correct them.

Stress can be caused by financial problems. Try to manage your budget carefully and seek advice and help if you're struggling – most universities have bursaries or hardship funds to help students with financial difficulties.

Emotional distress can also impact your mental health. During your tenure as an architecture student, it's possible you will experience difficult circumstances, such as physical illness or losing a relative, which are not always easy to overcome. Knowing that it's OK to ask for help if you're experiencing problems is a positive first step, as is finding the right channel for support. In terms of your education, universities understand that these events happen and have systems in place to help you. Unforeseen and severe cases can be assessed by the university and referred to as extenuating circumstances, often granting you additional time to complete work, or a delay to an examination. If you feel affected by such circumstances, you should ask the university to consider your case.

It may be that you don't wish to talk to a tutor who is involved closely with your academic progress, which is why schools will commonly have some other arrangement for student pastoral care. This can take the form of a personal tutor allocated at the start of the first year or a pastoral care tutor allocated to a year group, who can provide support and try to guide you through the extenuating circumstances, potentially recommending university counsellors and therapists. While it may feel like you're alone, there is a network of support within the university.

Peer-group support is important, and it's useful to remember that there will be others around you going through similar events and emotions. Try to talk to each other. Certain universities have hubs and peer-support programmes designed to offer advice and assistance in getting a healthier work-life balance. (See the appendix for more information on all of these matters related to mental health and managing stress.)

Five ways to get ahead

1. Develop an understanding of the ways an architect represents buildings in drawings (plan, section, elevation, isometric, axonometric, perspective).
2. Develop an understanding of simple building structure.
3. Develop your sketching ability by drawing buildings.
4. Learn how to use Photoshop.
5. Acquire some good books/reference materials on architectural history, theory and construction.

Second and third year

The difference between first year and second year

After completing first year successfully and embarking on a long university summer holiday, you should reflect on what you have been taught. Starting second year can feel that you are starting university again. Architectural tutors often see a certain forgetfulness when the autumn arrives and many put this down to the length of the academic summer recess. To avoid this happening, contemplate what you have learned in the previous academic year and continue to read architectural books, magazines and websites, look at buildings and exhibitions, and continue to draw and make. If you're so inclined, a summer job in practice is always a possibility.

The first thing when you return is to expect change, whether staff changes or new students. Experiencing this change can be good practice for becoming an architect, where no day is the same and you are continuously reassessing the decisions you made in previous days, communicating them to others and solving different problems. First year will have given you the confidence to work a little more swiftly and independently. The same lessons apply to managing your workload by keeping a consistent schedule and resisting falling behind as a result of displacement activity.

The sites and briefs tend to become more complex, with larger, more interconnected spaces, and you will develop a greater knowledge of architectural technologies. The transition will usually see you representing your ideas more effectively and more quickly.

While it's tempting to think 'the schedule for this first project is longer than I had in first year and the new academic year stretches far in front of me', aim to keep to the schedule and start work early. With some basic architectural skills mastered, second year courses require students to be more proactive in their learning and are a little looser, allowing students to bring some of their interests and preoccupations to their work.

3.1
Bartlett, University College London, Annabelle Tan Kai Lin, Condensed City, Year 2.
Second year should continue the spirit of exploration with form, colour and representation – yet also, a confidence with structure and materiality should begin to manifest itself.

All courses will require students to develop their time management skills – understanding the timing of the curriculum and what must be delivered when. Calendarising your assignments will give you a visible map of these academic commitments. The academic standard will also be higher, and the design studio will become the main focus of your activities.

Second year can be a difficult time psychologically, when you are neither a brand new first year nor a third-year finalist. The jump between years can be quite large, and you will probably be living away from university this year in shared accommodation with other students. Even if you've got a very small room in a student house, try to create a tidy desk space away from shared space and your housemates so design work is kept separate.

Shared domesticity can be difficult and requires tact, diplomacy and mutual support, which is also true when working in an architectural school's studio. There will be many distractions, and many requests for your company over coffee. The ability to concentrate on the problem at hand when all about you is in chaos is an architectural skill to develop. Coupled with this, the architectural problems you will be presented with will be more complex.

Briefs, sites, schedules of accommodation, types and volume of outputs and a higher standard together mean that many more design parameters will come into play. However, as you progress through the year, you will develop a more rigorous conceptual and intellectual grounding for your design and essay work, and your presentation techniques will improve, which is key to developing your architectural dexterity.

Robin Cross, architect and consultant for development in emerging countries, remembers his years of architectural education and notes that a predilection for highly finished presentation work could be detrimental to the time taken to achieve a depth of architectural understanding in project work, particularly in the early years: 'Too much focus on presentation for outside consumption in the first few years can be counterproductive. In the early years it's more important to get beneath the surface and spend time there. What is the most important thing to impart to students? The ambition and confidence to create the architecture of the future. And to create your own future.'

What will second year look like?

For a start, there will be more emphasis on design studio. All schools distribute academic credits according to the perceived importance of tasks/workload for a given subject and stage of architectural education. Here are a few example course structures to give you an idea of what to expect.

CURRICULUM EXAMPLE 1:

Design Studio (60 credits), Technology and Professional Practice (20 credits arranged in two separate tasks), Humanities (20 credits), and a space for an optional module which can be drawn from other creative disciplines in art, design and media (20 credits).
(Supplied by Ben Sweeting, Undergraduate Course Leader at the University of Brighton)

CURRICULUM EXAMPLE 2:

Design Projects (75 credits), Technology (15 credits), Practice (15 credits) and History and Theory (15 credits).
(From the Bartlett at University College London)

CURRICULUM EXAMPLE 3:

Contemporary Theories of Architecture (15 credits), Architectural Design 2: Exploration and Proposition (30 credits), Architectural Design 2: Resolution (30 credits), Introducing Architecture & Landscape Practice 2 (15 credits), Architecture Technology 2 (15 credits), History of Architecture and Landscape 2 (15 credits).
(From the University of Greenwich)

You will start to be able to blend insights from history, theory and technology classes into your design work and understand other concepts, such as how a roof meeting a wall has aesthetic and stylistic functions as well as the pragmatic ones of keeping out the cold and rain. All aspects of a building will start to come to mind, and how they relate to its whole – how it turns a corner, the rhythm of its fenestration or the elements that make up its staircase.

An architect must be consistent with their language and use of architectural elements, looking at the many historical examples. For example, Michelangelo's Laurentian Library in Florence took classical rules and reconfigured them, reversing protocols of void and mass, and utilising classical elements in the wrong places to develop a unique architectural treatment. This combined with his voluptuous staircase makes the whole conceptually rigorous. Another example is Carlo Scarpa, who used light, shadow, water, materiality of stone, metal and concrete to develop a language of his own which was truly original and sublime at all scales. For instance, how buildings turned a corner was a work in progress in the early Renaissance courtyard. Looking at the buildings themselves, you can see how architects were working out solutions over time, i.e. retaining even spacing and closing an arcade. It is only by looking at buildings in class and on building visits that you can observe architectural solutions, which are a starting point for design.

All architectural courses are different, but the scale of work will typically increase with each project. The following brief examples from second year illustrate the sorts of subjects and conversations that you will probably be having with your tutor. Second year consists of various scales of projects, from the domestic to the performative to the institutional.

Second year briefs and skills development

Schools do not have a common curriculum delivered at the same point in time. However, they do map the ARB criteria on to the shape of their courses. For example, some schools will deliver an understanding of urban design – the study of how cities have evolved, how people use them and how buildings old and new fit into them, particularly concerned with public space and placemaking – in their third year, while others will do this in second year, or spread throughout the undergraduate course. Schools usually build the complexity of brief/programme and site slowly, from small scale to larger scale. Each project is a microcosm of architectural ideas which are vital to understand at that point in the architectural education.

TERM 1 EXAMPLE BRIEF:

Design a house for real clients on a rural/suburban site.

The house is located on a site with a mature tree to one edge and open to neighbours on all four sides, and the clients are an architect and a painter – each needing their own studio as part of the house.

You will be asked to interview the clients to find out more about their way of life, their daily rituals and how they work. The lesson here is that understanding client needs is one of the most fundamental skills of an architect, as well as being able to open the client's eyes to the spatial opportunities afforded by the site and brief. Traditional domestic construction methods could also figure in this brief, and the lesson is to listen to the client's needs and have good, clear, graphic and verbal communication with them. As the year progresses, you will look at different structural and material choices to be made based on the nature and scale of the brief.

TERM 2 EXAMPLE BRIEF:

Design a small theatre in a gap site in a small town.

The theatre site has commercial party walls either side, and the brief is for a 350-seater auditorium, proscenium arch, fly tower, green room and box office, bar and cloakroom. The provision of the auditorium requires

3.2
University of Brighton, Eugene Kandinsky, model, Year 2.
The ability to transfer your propositions into structural models is a key skill to help the student understand the spanning potential of differing materials.

consideration of larger-span structures, acoustics, backstage access and the workings of fly towers. Equally, it requires the design of a performative episode of spaces that lead you to your seat in anticipation of the show, while also allowing swift and safe evacuation of the building.

One important first lesson is that the design must be inclusive and accessible. Furthermore, buildings don't simply exist in the brightness of daylight – they are diurnal, with the users and buildings subject to weather. A user also has the right to not do as you want them to do, which means there needs to be element of convenience involved in planning spaces. The flow of spaces and their interaction with the user should be seamless. Additionally, you may learn that the trabeated structural system of columns and beams is more appropriate in this context than masonry load-bearing construction.

TERM 3 EXAMPLE BRIEF:

Design a school on an urban London site.

The task here is to deliver a school situated on a derelict site at the centre of a relatively poor inner-city area. It is an island site, with roads on either side and complex urban conditions to resolve all around. You will be encouraged to explore not just the spaces required, day-to-day running and programmes of the school, but also to bring some intellectual preoccupation to the design (partioularly the urban design).

You might have been reading about system building, transience and the megastructural or kit of parts proposals for cities and buildings of the avant-garde architects of the 1960s. Your solution could depend on the provision of a series of elements and your own kit of parts. The important thing here is not how successful the design is particularly, but the merging in your work of history, theory and speculation about the future. You will be encouraged to reflect on ways and methods of teaching and learning (pedagogic methodologies) as a way to understand more about how you are being taught architecture.

3.3, 3.4
Birmingham City University,
Ahmed Hamid, Museum of Glassworks,
Year 2.
Second-year students should be
positing unusual configurations of
architecture and using what they
learned in first year. This project
artfully articulates 'void' and 'mass'.

Other schools have a more ad hoc or eclectic way of delivering the ARB
criteria for Part 1. For example, they can be 'unitised', and your unit may be
expected to follow the architectural preoccupations of your tutors. Briefs
are composed with the criteria in mind but their nature can change from
year to year. Some explore urban conditions on tight sites, while others
attempt to address the lack of affordable homes for first-time buyers in
cities by exploring micro-homes. Others reconsider the role of the library in
a contemporary context, with ubiquitous online access to information and
knowledge. Briefs could be lyrical or narrative, inspired by stories or myths.
Some start with the tectonics of building materials and their fabrication,
or by looking at cultures and traditions and social practices abroad and
importing them into local environments to provoke new ways of forming
social and architectural relationships. The scope of briefs is almost infinite.

Second year naturally increases in skill-level and many strides will be
made. You can go to bed grappling with an architectural problem and wake
up having solved it in the morning. Sometimes a sudden insight into the
nature of architecture occurs as a moment of epiphany.

A successful second-year design project negotiates the complex issues of
site, use, construction, aesthetics and delight with originality and creativity,
engaging in a concept or point of departure, an overriding reason of why
the project is designed the way it is. This may be urbanistically, related to
the choice of materials sympathetic to its surroundings, or creating public
space. There are also structural and constructional reasons – setting and
expressing structure and services external to the envelope of the building

69

(as in Hi-Tech architecture) to create free, unencumbered floorplates. Advances in technology can further influence decisions, making the most of graphene, or the Internet of Things, or digital fabrication. Again, the conceptual emphasis of a project can be almost infinite. A project is always judged on its rigorous pursuit in delivering its concept at all scales, from the context to the detail.

Ben Sweeting, Undergraduate Course Leader at the University of Brighton, offers some interesting insight into the perspective of a tutor on second year: 'I have always thought about the second year as the whole degree in one year: at the beginning you are effectively a first year and by the end you are a third year. We encourage different studios to focus on different methods, media and ways of looking, and use our shared working spaces and cross-studio events for peer learning between the groups. There is room in second year for students to learn different things in different orders, and projects can therefore be somewhat uneven in emphasis or media. The most obvious standout work is that which goes beyond this, anticipating the cohesion expected at third year.'

Undergraduate Design Tutor at Birmingham City University Bea Martin sums up the ethos of their second year and the teaching mechanisms they use to achieve this synthesis: 'Year two is about collaboration and professionalism. The two weeks' work placement together with Co.LAB – an innovative teaching module combining cross-disciplined projects – helps develop competency in group work as well as a "sneak peek" into the office environment. At this level, students are expected to recognise the elements of a project and their interdependence and develop their model and technical skills. At the end of Year 2, students are more inquisitive, show greater confidence, and tend to push boundaries.'

As an example, the Superstudio at Birmingham City University is a vertical studio that creates peer-learning opportunities as well as encouraging cross-school bonding, which is open to all students from first year to the final master's year in any creative courses at the university. It is a non-marked studio that explores architectural speaking, CAD clinics, detailing clinics, digital fabrication, 3D priniting, portfolio clinics and how to make a bilingual portfolio, as well as drones, architecture, virtual and augmented realities, and othor skills and concepts that allow students to experiment.

Why is history important?

As you progress from first year to second year, your knowledge of history and how it affoots what you see and experience today will typically increase, which will help in the design studio, as well as with historical essays and precedent studies. History will give you an insight into how the context of your sites for design projects has evolved over time, and will provide you with ideas on how to produce your work within an architectural context.

A broad knowledge of political, social, oral and cultural history and the awareness of their shifts over time is vitally important to an architect, and it's something you'll develop through Part 1. History impinges on all matters architectural, from the development of cities, to domestic space, public space, ritual, festivals, the typologies of buildings and their geographic position and materiality. Mark Garcia, researcher, writer and history and theory architecture tutor, feels that history and futurology/ future studies are indispensable to the fullest education of the 21st-century architect. He reflects: 'History is necessary to research, in order to stop, escape and to create it. History is the research into, through and for time, and because space–time is a single entity, to try to understand and act on space, you have to understand and try to act on time.'

The history of city development and its changing focus through time in particular cities is crucial, and each has a different story to tell. The key to initial settlement can be the shallowest crossing of a river, a defensive hill, a busy road from which to trade, or a fertile plain on which to farm or suchlike. Over time, the reasons for the development of the city changes, in some cases many times. These new imperatives change the metabolism of the city, including its internal organisation, perimeter, inhabitants, their skills, prosperity and relationship with other cities. For example, as technology changes over history, different raw materials are needed for fuel, building or transport. Imagine the great impact the car has had on the great American cities, and the cities where it was made, such as Detroit.

3.5
University of Coventry, Hadi Aaseem Pirmohamed, Mies Barcelona Pavilion model, Year 2.
The understanding of precedents is important to a fledgling architect's growth, and making models and drawings of others' work is a way of forging this understanding.

A knowledge of historical conflicts is also valuable for an architect. Cities have been strategic in times of war, and this imperative can have a massive impact on their development or demise. For example, much of Berlin was destroyed by bombing during and after the Second World War. This damage was further enhanced as Russian, American and other troops rushed to occupy it. Its subsequent partition into Communist East and capitalist West, the downfall of the Berlin Wall and the re-synthesis of Berlin's parts back together after 1989 have all left it with scars, geometries and creative opportunities peculiar to itself and inherently architectural. The bullet holes in older buildings and the route of the Berlin Wall are still visible in parts, as well as the memory of Checkpoint Charlie, which are all architectural conditions.

The social and demographic history of countries and cities is rich and complex. Cities can be open to those fleeing war or persecution, or they can be restrictive, riven along religious, caste, class or cultural lines to name by a few parameters that can define a city's social and geographical organisation and its divisions. The architect needs to understand these forces and any contestation they cause. This can happen at country and city scale, such as in Palestine, Cyprus or Berlin, but equally at street scale, such as the old sectarian divides at street level in Northern Ireland. Any architectural design in such areas needs to respond to these socio-political contexts. Any great historic city is a palimpsest of shifting boundaries, securities, enclosures and political machinations.

Architects must also understand the archaeology of cities and how building techniques have been influenced by place, culture, social interactions, historical governance, availability of building materials and the lifestyle of occupants over time. This enables you to retain the spatial grain and sense of place in proposals.

Religion and memorialisation of heroes and the proletariat equally affect the history and geometries of cities. Think of the Arc de Triomphe in Paris with its radiating boulevards, the medieval street plan of Canterbury in England with its central cathedral and, of course, the city-state of the Vatican in Rome.

Buildings also carry symbolic and semiotic architectural languages, which offer useful insights to an architect. Some are conditioned by religion, like the cathedral – great arks of hypertext storytelling for mostly illiterate worshippers. Classical architecture has its columnar orders, proportions and stylised allusions to timber construction with metopes and dentils, and so on. The representational column designed as a microcosm of the ideas held within a building has a rich tradition, and is stretched across time and culture in wonderful ways with hundreds of examples. All architectural elements including doors, windows, lavatories, staircases and handrail configurations have histories that are dependent on the available materials, skills of tradespeople, the wealth of the client, geographical location and cultural history.

Architectural style can be associated with the political and religious. For example, in Victorian Britain there existed the so-called 'Battle of the Styles', where Catholic architects developed extraordinary neo-gothic designs not only for churches, but also secular buildings such as law courts and town halls. They saw gothic as true, moral and pious,

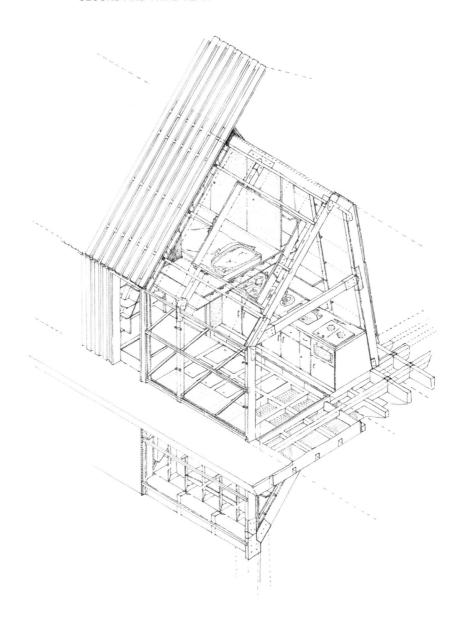

as opposed to the classical, which they saw as pagan and squalid. The
architectural press of the time relished the fight between neo-classical
architects and the neo-gothicists. The Houses of Parliament is a hybrid
result of these battles, consisting of a classical plan with gothic facades,
internal ornamentation and furnishings.

Art history is a tangled story, which often intersects with architectural
history, and knowledge of it can help clarify the main idea of a particular
period and its architecture. Often the word 'zeitgeist' is used to describe
the 'spirit of the age'. This can be felt across all of the arts, from
architecture to literature. Examples include the Arts and Crafts movement

73

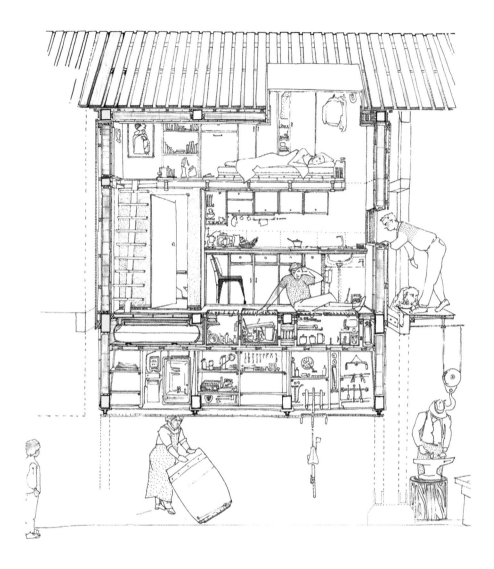

in England at the end of the 19th century, or the Symbolists mainly in Paris at the same time, or the initial development of European Modernism at the Bauhaus in Germany in the 1920s and 1930s.

Understanding the history of technology and its genealogy is valuable for architects, because it provides sound examples of how the development of technology can profoundly change architectural form. This metamorphic relationship is as true today as it was then. Students should take note, for example, of the technology of the flying buttress and its contribution to medieval architecture – particularly, how it made the gothic high nave possible. Furthermore, consider the impact the introduction of the lift has had on the topology of New York, or the development of large sheets of glass on Modernist buildings, and hence the importance of transparency in the architectural lexicon.

3.7
London South Bank University, Muneeb Kahn, Displacement Home: A Cluster of Micro Homes, Year 3. **During second year a student should be developing a much more detailed understanding of how different elements of buildings go together, how floors meet walls and how walls meet roofs.**

Why is theory important?

It's useful to increase your knowledge of theory of architecture in second and third year. Theory is often the unseen force behind what an architect designs, and it embodies their political, social and spatial preoccupations, which means the development of a theoretical position for deployment in design studio is valuable to your projects.

Good architecture will have reasons behind it, and it's not simply a response to make an architectural product that satisfies a need to earn money. You should reflect on why you make decisions, and your priorities in relation to your intellectual point of departure. Architecture does not come from nothing, and a personal way of going about this is helped by being aware of the numerous theories of architecture. Theories of architecture are synonymous with the times in which they are formulated. And as times, technologies and philosophies change, they can become outdated. When this occurs, architects can be accused of stubbornly sticking to dogma and doctrine no longer appropriate for the modern world. An example of this are pseudo-Georgian office blocks, where an architect is convinced that the architecture of the 18th century is a good model for a 21st-century office block, which creates an anomalous architectural hybrid, out of step with its time and function.

Architectural theories are mostly developed by bringing something from outside architecture into architectural discourse. This could be a philosophy, an admiration of contemporary technology, or a scientific or mathematical insight. A useful example is Jacques Derrida's 'deconstruction' theories in philosophy. This theory was adopted by architects, architectural critics and theorists in the 1980s to describe some of the most daring architectural designs of the period. An exhibition, Deconstructivist Architecture, was mounted at the Museum of Modern Art in New York, and the exhibition catalogue made much of linking Deconstructivism with Russian Revolutionary Constructivism. This was a clever but erroneous conflation of philosophies, political action and architectural imperatives. The seven architects exhibited (Daniel Libeskind, Zaha Hadid, OMA, Frank Gehry, Peter Eisenman, Coop Himmelb(l)au, Bernard Tschumi) had all developed their work in different ways, and none were particularly interested in Derrida's philosophy of deconstruction.

Furthermore, architectural styles (materials/techniques) become fashionable at certain periods in time. Groups of architects form around fashionable theories, formal tropes and aesthetic fetishes. Such fashionable work can quickly infect architecture schools, and a generation of students can develop very similar architectural affectations. You must therefore interrogate and be critical of the theories you are being exposed to. Examples include the Brutalists in the United Kingdom during the 1950s and 1960s, the Metabolists in Japan during the 1960s and 1970s, or the global outbreak of Postmodernism in the late 1970s and 1980s. Each group has a theory of how they believe the world to be or a theory

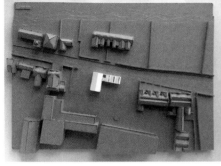

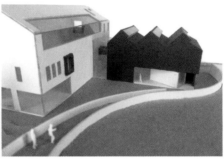

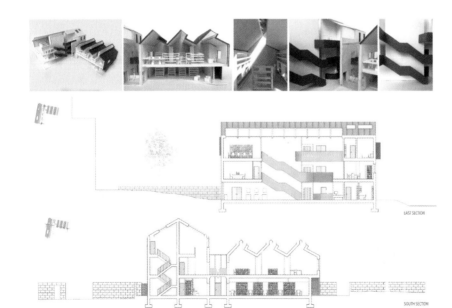

EAST SECTION

SOUTH SECTION

3.8, 3.9
University of Strathclyde, Mary Leak,
Library, St Andrews, Year 2.
**A wider understanding of the
importance of context, urban massing
and urban grain should be illustrated in
second-year proposals.**

of how technology will change buildings/living standards/human society in the future. Architectural aphorisms abound – these are short sayings that some architects use as mantras, with most created during the 20th century and linked to the development of Modernism. Examples include Adolf Loos's 'Ornament is crime' and Mies van der Rohe's 'Less is more'. Architectural dogma can become limiting as well as an inspiration – so try to remain critical and ask what is excluded in pursuing any given architecture or theory.

There are theories of perception, theories and science of neural cognition, and colour theories, which can all influence architecture too. Some architects have a preoccupation with the colour blue, others with all primary colours, and others still with millennial pink. Reflect on the reasons why light green is often used in hospitals, and its soothing effect. Light, shade and shadow can also be used in a more phenomenological way. As architect Ian Ritchie remarked: 'Understanding that architecture has more than a utilitarian or aesthetic function, and how it interacts with all our senses, has the potential to transform design and engineering: of architecture, cities, objects and our environment. Our brains drive our behaviour. Architects are facing the reality that communication between the buildings and spaces that we design and their users is something dynamic – a non-stop relationship that can change us for good or ill.'

There is a long line of theories about urban planning, city development, urban morphology and the syntax of urban space, as well as theories of townscape, public space and placemaking. Architects have designed cities or large districts of cities that illustrate their own theories of the urban. Some of the theories are turned into precise plans for urban utopias conditioned by their architects' political and social beliefs, such as Le Corbusier's Ville Radieuse, or Oscar Niemeyer et al.'s Brasília. Meanwhile, others speculate in prose and drawings about the anatomies of cities, which can be empirical or lyrical. An example of the latter is Colin Rowe's and Fred Koetter's *Collage City* (1978), which puts the case that cities evolve over time, making them palimpsests of forms, streets, urban densities and technologies refigured over different eras, and that the great joy of a city is an unexpected clash or juxtaposition of these conditions.

The Surrealist city, similar to the Collage City, is a massive engine of chance throwing up disparate objects and ideas but fuelled by desires brought together to form a continual dynamism. The Surrealists believed the city was a psychic text to be read, explored and excavated – a landscape of dreams, nightmares and uncanny-ness. To the Situationists, who came next, Paris was a maelstrom of ambiances and situations to be experienced during wandering *derives.* Architecture has been developed out of both theories of the same city.

As architectural representations become more dynamic and embrace time through animation, and virtual and augmented reality, then it's also helpful to understand film theory. A long list of films and directors have explored a myriad of techniques about the speed of jump-cuts, the points of view of multiple camera angles, and the permeability of architectural boundaries such as walls, doors and floors. The choreography of architecture's performative possibilities over time, storyboarding and the episodic has become part of architectural theory.

You must start to develop your own theories. These might be driven by technology, philosophy, art, phenomenology or a mixture of these ideas. It is difficult to do this unless you are aware of what has gone before in terms of history and theory. Build up your own canon of references, precedents of buildings and writing that you feel echo your intellectual and design interests. Develop views on the nature of the contemporary city; its populations, culture and architecture. Once you have done this, reflect on how your architecture fits within this meta-architecture of theories.

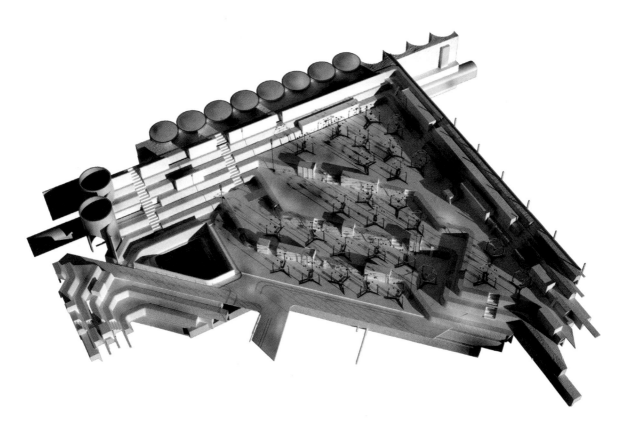

Technology and the future

Architects are in the business of speculating about the future. Even the most reactionary architects take time to procure sites, and buildings of any size can take years to design and build. Speculations made by consultancy teams concern the price of raw materials, politics, change of governments, projected inflation rates and lead-in times for elements such as steel.

9.10
Bartlett, University College London, Grey Grierson, Negotiation of States, Year 3.
Modelling skills, whether analogue or virtual or a hybrid, should progress as the course progresses. The ability to swiftly model and explore a concept in three or four dimensions is crucial to an architect's success.

TECHNOLOGY AND DESIGN

Technology is the pragmatic means with which we realise our buildings. Design studio will test and develop your dexterity with ideas of ventilation, joining disparate materials together, making stable foundations and spanning roofs. As you progress through the course, build your knowledge of the different ways to achieve these and other pragmatic solutions. Over time, you can become more creative with these solutions, to mirror the concepts in your designs as technologies continue to evolve.

Even for the most experienced architects, the way they work will have changed since they were at university. It is an exponential curve, which is becoming steeper year on year. Architect Peter Fotheringham, whose career has spanned both sides of the architect/client divide, as well as historical refurbishment and radical newbuilds, makes an observation about the dynamic: 'In the 1970s architects were lead designers and project managers, dealing directly with the client and main contractors on traditional contracts. This pivotal role has been changed by the complexity of design, the growth of specialisation within the professions, and new forms of contract. The architect is still fundamental to the design process, but the profession has to keep evolving to maintain its relevance. Change is all-consuming.'

Materials change, and the palette of materials available to architects is becoming more diverse, such as shape-memory plastics. Materials can be digitally fabricated using additive printers, subtractive milling machines or laser cutters, and robots on building sites are becoming much more common. 3D scanners are used to survey both existing buildings and those under construction, while global positioning system (GPS) satellites can allow us to pinpoint where we are, or the positioning of building elements, with precise accuracy. Geographic information systems (GIS) can superimpose digital maps of areas of geology, archaeology, human settlement and water tables at the press of a button and represent them as 3D models. Computation can be embedded into the more inert materials to sense stresses in concrete bridges and make walls and floors responsive to human movement, to name but two examples. Fundamentally, students are encouraged to acknowledge these developments and to experiment – to make test pieces, proof-of-concept models and partial 1:1-scale elements.

New building typologies emerge with new technologies. Medical operating theatres have evolved as the technology within them has changed, and 'clean rooms' for building electronics are now commonplace. For example, contemporary technologies have given us the digital, robotic, internet shopping distribution centres and high-security server farms.

Different technologies also have different locational needs. The online shopping hub, or fulfilment centre, is ideally at the intersection of motorways, and the server farm perhaps near large bodies of water for cooling purposes and security. Meanwhile, older technologies such as oil and gas platforms can be repurposed to provide secure, offshore server hubs for those wishing to store data outside a specific country's jurisdiction – as has happened in the small principality of Sealand off the coast of the UK. The mining of Big Data is now commonplace, able to show us changing trends in demographics, or traffic flows across a city in real time, and it can even show us medical statistics.

ETHICS

The issue of ethics is crucial. As the world becomes more linked and our personal data more exposed and potentially used against us, an ethical framework will be required within which these technologies can operate for our benefit, not to our detriment. This ethical conundrum will be exacerbated by technologies that are still embryonic. Stem-cell medical interventions and the growing of human organs, synthetic biology and the making of artificial biological living cells and nanotechnology will all have the potential to change, augment and sensitise human and animal bodies in different ways. If, for example, our fingertips become more sensitive through some technology, our haptic sensations – via which we experience our environment – change and therefore so does our architecture. This is a basic but useful example to consider. The body and its senses are the conduit through which we experience and relate to architecture, and if the bandwidth and scale of that body changes, many more architectural experiences are open to us, both good and bad.

Some philosophers, cultural theorists and geographers describe our age as the 'Anthropocene'. While humanity was not part of the formation of climate dynamics and rock formations in previous geomorphic eras, it now is. Humanity's impact on the ecological state of our planet is increasing at an alarming rate. New plastic continents, mining scarring, machine landscapes with no human habitation, non-sustainable farming, massive urbanism, pollution and toxic dumping and landfill have created a world beyond nature. It's imperative that architects think about the effects of a design on the environment and ecology.

In practice you can't separate history, theory and futures, which is why it's a valuable lesson for students to learn early and conceptualise within their projects and designs. The knowledgeable, experienced architect will create designs that read the city and a building's site, and posit architectures that are symbiotically at one with context in terms of history, theory, tectonics, environment and semiotics. Architectural tutor John Bell concludes: 'Technology is inseparable from architectural design. It is, in my view, anachronistic and misguided to separate it from other aspects of studio.'

0.11
University of Brighton, Agata Malinowska, aerial view of city precinct, Year 3. There are different ways to present work; some are analogue and hand-drawn, some hyper-real using the computer. Others, such as this, use the computer but in a stylised way to produce an almost comic-book vivaciousness.

Landscape and reducing the carbon footprint: greening your building

Architectural students also need to understand concepts of sustainability, and how a building can utilise green technologies to reduce its carbon footprint. This carbon footprint starts way before a building is on site, depending on where materials are sourced. You should find out whether they are sustainable and weigh up the many factors. The way operatives, the design team and later users make their way to the building are all factors in a carbon footprint calculation, as well as insulation, window areas and type of glazing or green roofs, along with many other parameters. Here is a list of points when considering your design sustainably.

1. Architecture is a sub-set of landscape, not the other way around. Consider your architecture as contributing to the wider landscape and its impact, and how it can mitigate the effects of climate change. There are many tactics that range from walking/using public transport on site visits, and designing in sustainable urban drainage systems, to using photovoltaic cells. Many technological systems are also being developed in this respect, and the likes of synthetic biology might be able to help.

2. An ongoing architectural imperative is to design 'resilience' into sites, buildings, communication routes and infrastructure across cities. This means using architecture or engineering to design protection from the ravages of flood, bush fires or communication breakdown,

3.12
University of Coventry, Eva Chung, Knowledge Exchange Centre, Year 3.
It is a good idea to depict users in your drawings and models; they can give a sense of the vitality, user experience and scale of your architectural intent.

whether electronic or transport-related. The resilience of cities is also financial and social, and needs to be thought about holistically. Many successful student projects, for example, have speculated on the effects on London when the sea level rises. These may feature happy punters moving through the city on gondolas, passing by houses on stilts – but what happens to the submerged or partially flooded houses, shops and offices, and the people who use them? Consider the severe diseases that could spread if all the sewers flood and there is raw sewage floating around.

3. There are many established ways to create greener architecture. Some of the most established are taught to us through the centuries; look at the orientation of buildings and their design to optimise environmental phenomena. For example, courtyard fountains in hot climates, the use of shading devices and cross-ventilation are in most cases more agreeable than air-conditioning, but this depends on the use of space and the need for security.

4. The storage, production, economic dissemination and recycling of urban water is another major issue. As we use more and more water in unsustainable ways, methods need to be developed that stem this profligacy. For example, grey water systems are now commonplace, as is water filtration through reed beds.

5. Think about the word 'sustainable' – a word so ubiquitous in its use by architects and others that it has nearly lost its meaning. Sustainable is defined as a method of harvesting or using a resource so that the resource is not depleted or permanently damaged, for example sustainable techniques, or sustainable agriculture, or referring to a sustainable lifestyle or society.

6. Cities and buildings develop their own microclimates, depending on their topology and materiality. Microclimates are highly complex and change over time. When you design a piece of architecture, you insert it within this ecology of climatic phenomena and you change it. Your architecture should mitigate a microclimate's bad effects and use its good effects to reduce the carbon footprint. For example, if a building catches wind, convert it into electricity and sell it back to the grid.

7. Your building might utilise urban agriculture or animal husbandry. Green roofs can be constructed that support soil (this obviously affects the structure of your building, as large amounts of wet mud are heavy) but benefits can include harvesting your own fruit and vegetables – you may even have a pig or two on the roof.

8. The way to create green walls is to create a vertical layer of plants both within and outside buildings. Lighting and irrigation systems have been developed to sustain internal green walls. Buildings are becoming bioreactors, and south-facing facades of microalgae,

3.13
University of Greenwich, Stockwell Street,
green roof.
The aim of this roof is to provide
a dry Mediterranean-type garden,
responding to the increase in urban
temperatures and to provide social
and teaching space.

enclosed in hollow glazing, have been developed. Microalgae is similar in size to bacteria, but can produce copious amounts of biofuel. The algae also provides sound and heat insulation, and it is fed on piped carbon dioxide. As the sun becomes more seasonally intense, the algae will grow denser and can be harvested and fermented to produce biogas. The warm water that the algae grows in can also be stored to provide heat in the colder seasons.

9.   Aquaponics is another method of producing food that may be much more extensively used in the future. Large vats of water with added nutrients filled with fish (edible tilapia is a good example), vegetables and herbs are grown on the surface of the vats, with plant roots feeding on nothing but the water and nutrients created from re-circulated fish excrement that has been broken down by nitrifying bacteria.

10. Green roofs can be planted with any number of plants, landscape styles and ecologies, and can feature ponds, or even beehives to provide honey. While greening the roofscape of a building, roof gardens offer invaluable opportunities for innovative architectural design.

3.14
University of Greenwich,
Aquaponics Laboratory.
**Asian vegetables (tarot, amaranth,
bitter gourd and sessile joyweed)
being grown in the Aquaponics Lab.**

3.15
University of Greenwich, Green Roof.
**The secret garden contains
Mediterranean-type shrubs as well as
espaliered apple and pear trees.**

As a student you should also speculate on emerging technologies that might offer capability for constructing carbon-neutral or even carbon-negative buildings in the future. Try to learn to use Building Information Modelling (BIM), which will help you test your assumptions about the environmental conditions of your architecture.

Third year (full-time) or fourth year (part-time)

In contrast to second year, third (or fourth) year involves more self-reliance and questioning in essays, design studios and tutorials. Students find that they develop a clearer ambition for their design work and feel more comfortable in their ability to implement a variety of skills and concepts in achieving them. This final-year work can be used to show off your skill to their best advantage, to smooth your entry into the architectural profession.

Once you've got the previous year passed and out the way, it's important to start preparing for the subsequent year. Most courses are predicated on the students producing what in some places is called a 'comprehensive design project (CDP)' and a lengthy essay or dissertation. This allows students to research and deepen their knowledge by bringing their interests and preoccupations in to develop an intellectual agenda that ideally manifests itself in both written and drawn work over a sustained period of months. Some schools let final-year students choose their own sites and programmes for this large final project, while others don't.

The marks for your whole degree will be weighted towards these outputs in the final year, so you want to be ready when the first term commences. The final undergraduate year is about deepening knowledge and expanding architectural interests, as well as developing new areas of focus.

Subjects and tuition for the written element of your final year are often agreed before the end of the second year. This is to give students maximum time to research and gather information that might be important and start to plan an argument, narrative arc and structure. More often than not that a successful dissertation has a synergy with your final CDP, which means the research or information you gather will help you prepare for both the writing and the design project. Try to follow your interests and intellectual preoccupations in choosing subjects for both design and writing. When researching always reference your sources, and write footnotes as you are writing the main text, while also remembering that primary research sources are valuable.

3.16
Dundee University, Imagined City, model installation, Year 3.
The city is an amalgam of disparate forms, materials, plot sizes, planning regulations and typological profiles. It is this diversity of architectural taxonomy that gives each city is unique and recognisable skyline.

Deciding on what you might do in writing and design is a matter of strategic importance. This may be the first time you have been allowed to set an intellectual agenda of your own so try to make the most of it; however, it's best to avoid areas where you have little knowledge and experience.

For the design, you will need access to people, briefing documentation and site knowledge, which means you should avoid inaccessible sites or building types where you have no access to precedents. Sometimes it is a good idea to find a person or an organisation to act as a notional client, as this can grant you access to briefing information, precedent studies and potential appropriate sites. A 'client' can also be a good, knowledgeable, sounding board to help you hone your ideas.

Brief writing is an architectural skill in itself. Make sure the brief you write for yourself is detailed and based on the study of precedents or a full understanding of the processes to be housed in your building. A common pitfall for students is that their briefs lack pragmatic substance such as schedules of accommodation, bubble diagrams of the relationships between particular spaces or the environmental conditioning required for certain spaces.

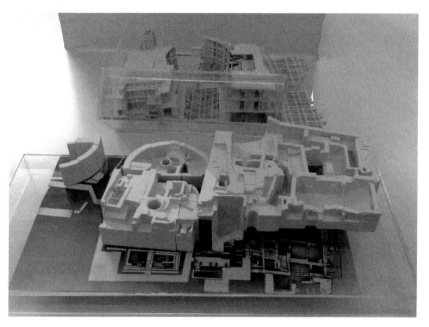

3.17
London South Bank University, Waad Darzi, model.
Some projects are a complex series of formal responses, almost like watch parts – clicking into place, highly articulated to their unique position in the urban fabric or within the building itself. This produces a variation of architectural pieces and a multi-scaled sense of space and enclosure.

Often students, enlivened by this newfound freedom, choose greenfield sites for their final project. While occasionally appropriate, this can be a poor decision because most successful architecture fits in and augments its context. One of the things you will be judged on is your ability to do this, and the rarefied relationships of brownfield urban sites offer a greater opportunity to show how you can resolve such issues. How you respond to townscape and urban fabric is important, and will usually make your designs more successful. Get all of the above sorted early, preferably over the summer before your final year. It's not uncommon for students to waste the first term engaged in gathering information and displacement activity, which can cause stress later. Plan ahead and try to spread the work evenly.

You will sometimes be asked to provide a distinct technical report or drawings as part of the final project. As you tailor your building to its site and resolve its functional content, you will need to learn how to pose the right questions to consultants and tutors. Your building will be different from everyone else's and you will need to ask different questions. Again, the ability to ask such questions is an architectural skill, linked to the ability to see the ramifications and consequences (and indeed creative opportunities) of the answers you receive.

As Birmingham City University tutor Bea Martin states: 'The final year is fuelled by critical thinking. Pushing students to delve into the "immaterial". [At BCU] one single project is taken from exploration to resolution. This includes methods, theories and processes that define conceptual architecture to be resolved with technical ingenuity. At the end of the year, students can integrate the imaginative and technical manipulation of form, the ability to draw inspiration from a broad body of knowledge, and to discover their own identity through how they communicate and represent their work. Students reach their Part 1 with a sense of duty and committed to "take on" the challenges posed by contemporary society.'

The project you finish will be the most complex, detailed and best represented project you have done to date, and your crits will have rehearsed you in how to introduce the site, client, programme and intellectual points of departure, and to swiftly link this with your written work and your solution.

Some schools afford the opportunity to meet and talk through your project with an external examiner at the end of the academic year, which is seen as a rite of passage. The role of the external examiner varies between schools, but in most they are there to check that the student cohort has been marked appropriately. Highly experienced external examiner Professor Murray Fraser from UCL's Bartlett School of Architecture comments: 'The crucial thing that schools can teach undergraduate students is how to think for themselves, and thus how to find their own ways of research for projects and essays. This is what an outstanding Part 1 student is able to do – and what I look for in the interview.'

Finally, enjoy graduation day – you have achieved something valuable!

Five ways to get ahead

1. Develop your architectural interests and preoccupations. Acquire more specific books/references that reflect your architectural interests.
2. Look more closely about how buildings fit into their urban environment, at the large scale, but also at the small scale.
3. Become more aware of architectural technology, how things go together and how they stand up. Experiment with computer-aided design (CAD) packages.
4. Experiment with designing using a clear concept that orders your design and details (a simple example being an interweaving of interior and exterior space).
5. Develop a more finely tuned understanding of history, theory and technology.

3.18
University of Greenwich,
Alexander Wilford, Smithfield Lorry Depot,
Year 3.
As students near the end of their final
undergraduate year, they are often
allowed to develop their own brief and
find a site for it. They are also allowed
to indulge their interests outside
architecture. This project was an ideal
agenda for a 'petrol head'.

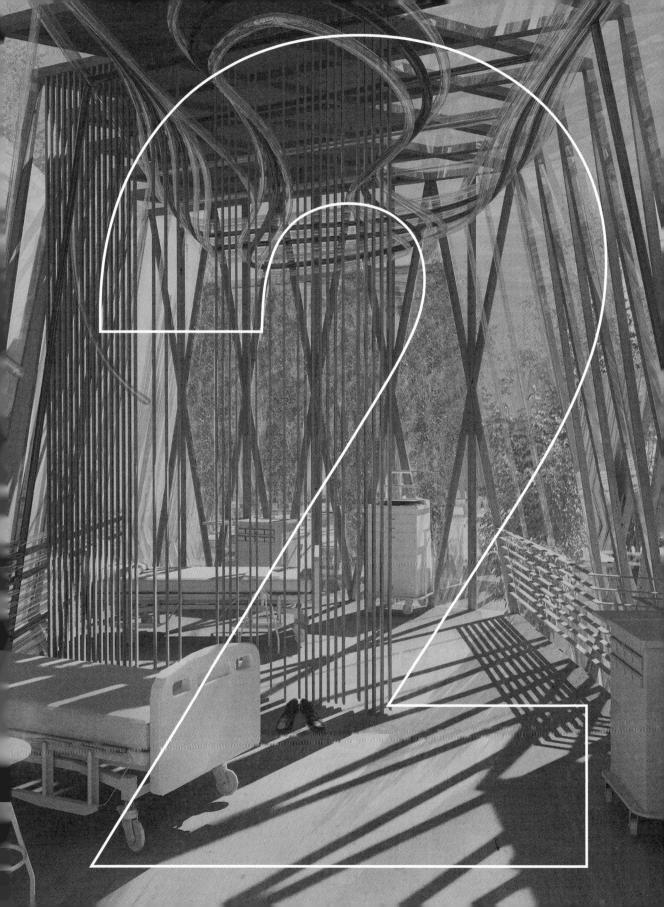

93 **Year(s) out and working
in an office**
111 **MArch and Part 2**

POSTGRADUATE

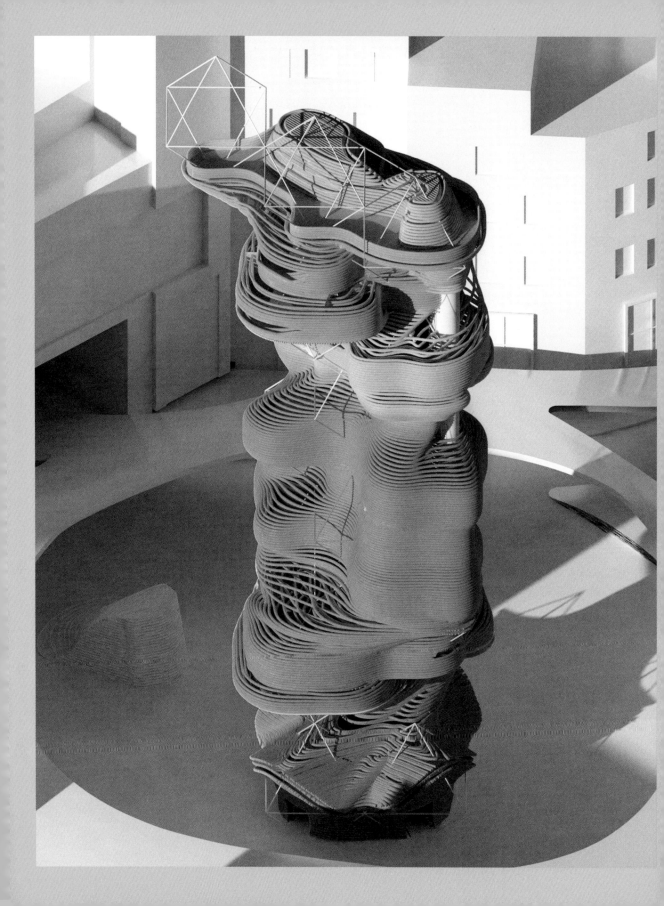

Year(s) out and working in an office

Preparing for year(s) out

The year(s) out working in an architectural practice is an important phase between undergraduate and postgraduate study. While architectural schools are excellent for developing skills, they cannot replicate the experience architectural students gain in practice. The experience of working on real projects with consultants, clients, developers, planners, builders and other statutory authorities, as well as working in teams with other architects, is usually your first taste of what life might be like after full qualification.

This chapter is designed to help you find vacancies, prepare a portfolio, shine at interview, stay in touch with your school, record and learn from your experiences, and develop a receptive mind in practice to maximise your learning opportunities.

FIRST STEPS

The so-called 'year out' can be longer than a calendar year; it will often start in June and run until September of the following year. One of the first things to do is ensure your CV is up to date. To help you do this:

- Ask your school to show you examples of successful CVs.
- Attend any available workshops to improve your own.
- Seek the help of employability staff or the Student Union.

Practices will be most interested in your architectural skills, so make sure you bring these skills and experiences to the fore. Write a short but enthusiastic, engaging covering letter on why you want the job within this practice (research the practices you apply to first). It's also effective to include a few, but not too many, images of your architectural work. Some practices will also have their own standard application process, separate from a CV or letter, with a set of specific questions and requests.

An important source of vacancies is the RIBA's job board (jobs.architecture.com). Rupesh Vara, Job Board Sales Manager at the RIBA, offers useful advice to students seeking year-out positions: 'For many Part 1 students, seeking a work placement for practical experience during their year out is daunting. It might be the first time that they've had to write a CV, attend a formal interview or show their portfolio to a potential employer. How do they even get started and seek out a suitable workplace? There are lots of options in terms of finding the right practice;

4.1
University of Greenwich, Owen Nagy, Artist's Studio of the Future, Year 3. **This proposition examines the accommodation needs for artists of the future, their way of life and their use of future technologies.**

many students look at magazine job sites or their schools have established contacts. At the RIBA, we have a job board platform – RIBA Jobs – that gives chartered practices the opportunity to post jobs. This enables jobseekers and students from all over the UK to view roles online – many of which are advertising for Part 1 and Part 2 students.'

Below are some top tips on how Part 1 students can ensure they stand out from the crowd and make a lasting impression when they set about writing that first CV:

- Choose the right format and ensure your CV is tailored for the company you are applying to.
- Use the job description as a guide, identifying key words and phrases you can weave into your CV.
- Highlight your transferable skills: draw on life experiences, and examples of completing recent work.
- Remember to include a cover letter.
- Focus on hobbies and interests: you could really use this to stand out, for example by detailing travel, which would show you are comfortable in new environments.
- Remain true to your experiences and qualifications.
- Edit and proofread: make sure you check for typos and grammatical errors.
- Include supporting examples.

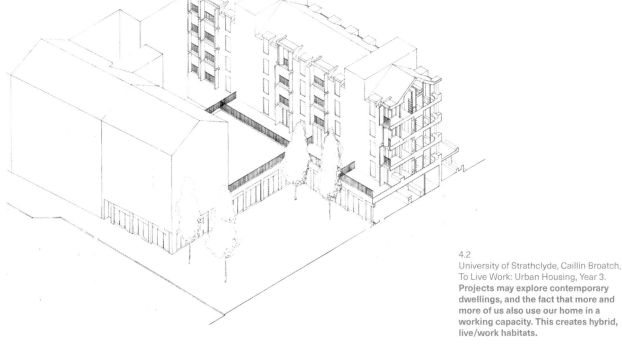

4.2
University of Strathclyde, Caillin Broatch, To Live Work: Urban Housing, Year 3. Projects may explore contemporary dwellings, and the fact that more and more of us also use our home in a working capacity. This creates hybrid, live/work habitats.

Applying for jobs

ROUTES INTO PRACTICE

Start looking around, and inform practices or agencies that you are looking for a year-out job. Also be aware of adverts placed in publications and webzines such as the *Architects' Journal, Building Design* and *Dezeen.* There are many different avenues for seeking work:

- Practices may get in touch with architectural school staff asking for recommendations of students, or may send adverts directly to the school.
- You can talk to the Part 3 coordinator at your school (if it has one), as they will often be aware of opportunities.
- Practices can invite students to interview if they have admired their work at end-of-year shows, or external examiners may offer a student a job after their external examination.
- You can apply to an architectural job agency, which will ask for a copy of your CV and typically seek an interview before putting you on its books. It will be particularly interested in your previous office experience, if you have any. This could result in quick, varied experience. It might not have the benefits of a longer-term tenure at a supportive practice, but could be more lucrative in the short term.
- You can apply to practices you want to work for on the off-chance. Practices occasionally have vacancies that are not advertised, or need to bulk up their numbers as a new project has unexpectedly arrived. Even if practices don't have any vacancies, they may keep your application on file.
- You can look for work abroad, applying to an overseas RIBA practice. (This is important, as a practice's familiarity with RIBA-validated architectural education and membership of the RIBA is needed for signing off your practice experience record.) Working abroad will broaden your experience and, depending where you are, open you up to other conceptions of architecture in different climates, cultures and construction industries.

Remember that the process of applying for jobs is not always easy, and you are not alone if you experience frustration. It can be a worrying period, and unfortunately some students do fail to find a job, which sets back progress to Part 2 and 3. If this is the case, be assured that it is not necessarily a reflection on your ability or potential, and can simply be the result of misfortune. The best way to manage is to simply ensure that you're prepared for the process, so at least you'll know you've done everything possible to find a job.

Peter Morris, architect and Founding Director of AHMM, reports on how his practice sources year-out students: 'We target specific end-of-year shows, and we also benefit from word-of-mouth recommendations, both from friendly academics and recent graduates already working at AHMM. We also receive a large quantity of speculative applications.'

Peter Fotheringham, says: 'Different schools prepare students differently and prospective students should be aware that this initial training is a preparation for practice. They do not enter the workplace as fully formed project architects; they will effectively serve an apprenticeship. Initially try to work in a practice that offers a range of projects to engage with. Prepare yourself for the role and look for what keeps you fully engaged, knowing that things will change.'

FINDING THE RIGHT PRACTICE

As when researching architecture schools, it's worth doing due diligence on architectural offices, because offices are as varied as the different personalities that work in them. There are large, corporate, commercial practices and small niche ones, as well as the whole spectrum in between. Check out their work, where they've appeared in the professional press and the awards they've won, if any.

Where possible, try to find out the general impression of the practice within the profession. Do they mentor students well? Do they pay their interns? Are office members happy in each other's company? Do they have a good social life? Is there laughter, or is everyone working silently so they can leave swiftly in the evening? It's important to assess your own preferences when it comes to the type of practice you want to work with. The process of finding a year-out position should be an ambitious and proactive series of choices on your part.

Preparing your portfolio

Your office interview portfolio will differ from your academic portfolio, and it should be more succinct, even more architectural. Weight the contents of your portfolio towards the latter part of your studies, including any office experience. Be selective and succinct with your portfolio choices, filtering for quality and value to the interview.

When asked to Interview by an office, aim to be smart, punctual and attentive. An architectural office interview is different from an architectural school interview insofar as a school interview is predominantly based on analysing your ability to learn and your creative potential. Whereas an office interview is about ascertaining what skills you have, how you might fit into the team, your experience of the real world and your ability to cope with it.

To prepare for interview, consider your answers to the following common questions:

4.3
Haworth Tomkins Architects, studio.
When you apply and are interviewed for an office job, you are applying to join a small community of professionals.

- What experience have you had in an architect's office, and how long were you there?
- What projects were you involved in, and at what stage?
- What did you learn?
- What experience have you had working in teams?
- Have you any site experience?
- Why do you want to work for this practice?
- What do you know about this practice and its architectural philosophy?
- What are your architectural interests?
- Which buildings do you admire, and why?

Aim to answer questions directly and arrive at the architectural point. Peter Morris describes his company's interview format: 'Two members will interview each candidate, one of whom will be an associate director. The portfolio is the principal focus for the interview, but the interview is as much about what is said as what is shown.' He also describes what they look for in a Part 1 year-out candidate: 'A desire to learn; a willingness to take on responsibility; a good eye; the ability to articulate an idea in words and on paper; a range of drawing skills; enthusiasm for architecture; curiosity about the world; intelligence; energy.'

Peter Fotheringham says he looks for 'intelligence and the ability to absorb, communicate and empathise'. Other offices can have a different take on what they look for, depending on their focus. For example, Ian Ritchie works as an architect with a more international focus and in his practice they look for '[students with] a foreign language (music as a possible substitute) to demonstrate a broader cultural understanding, and [they] must have hand-made something complex, full-scale, which someone else has used. Beyond technology, the haptic and political side of architecture is very important in our office.'

Deferrals and academic currency

If you are a part-time student, you will continue to study and move on to master's level while working. Having completed Part 1 in architecture, you will have an undergraduate degree, which is a broad qualification.

Deferring your return to academic studies after Part 1 can happen for a range of reasons – financial, emotional, health – and it is sometimes necessary for a combination of reasons. Often students return to school after a deferral with a clearer, more life-experienced head.

While architectural education is not cheap, and the need to generate income with a salary is important, there is also such a thing as 'academic currency'. If you are a full-time student considering whether to defer returning to university for more than a couple of years, you should assess the decision carefully. Things can change swiftly in schools, and what you have learned previously may no longer be contemporary when you return. Students who spend long periods away from university architectural education often find it hard to adapt when they return.

It can be a trade-off between these two notions. Many people have decided after Part 1 that a career in architecture is not for them, and have gone on to successful careers in a range of creative professions: interior design, landscape architecture, urban design, masterplanning, planning, architectural technology, product design, graphic design, lighting design, set design or various others.

4.4
Cullinan Studio, Tow Path Garden.
Some offices tend their own garden as part of office duties. A garden can be a calming influence on office life.

PEDR

Once you have started your year (or years) out post-Part 1 and post-Part 2, you must register on the RIBA Professional Experience and Development Record (PEDR), which becomes an important document when you sit your Part 3. It's an online system that allows you to record and reflect on your experience. It can be difficult to remember exactly what you have done in a fast-moving office environment months later, so try to update it at regular intervals. At Part 3 level, the PEDR is used to ascertain your levels of experience in all the constituent activities a qualified architect must have.

You will also need to have a professional studies advisor (PSA) from your school, or alternatively the RIBA offers a fee-based PEDR monitoring service for students without a PSA (see the appendix). Tony Clelford, PSA and Director of Part 3 at the University of Greenwich, defines the role: 'It's the school's point of contact with the graduate (who may/may not also be a student). The PSA signs off the student's PEDR, offers support on professional development (either via the PEDR or some other link such as recall visits, email newsletters, alumni links) and provides a sounding board (and sometimes a safety net) in terms of major professional, developmental, employment problems. They also offer advice on salaries and the employment market in different sectors/locations.'

While filling in your PEDR, try to show that you are meeting the criteria for Part 3 experience and knowledge. There are fees for signed-off sheets and registration on the PEDR website, and you can ask your office if they will pay these. (Further information provided in the appendix.)

Office life

TASKS

Working in an office is an excellent way to learn about more of the day-to-day practice of an architect, which is typically more prosaic than the fantasy image of the super-architect sketching landmark buildings on the serviettes in fine-dining establishments.

Be eager and willing to experience a wide variety of tasks, and don't be afraid to make it known if you feel you are not receiving enough mentorship, or if you have been stuck with the same simple tasks for months.

Architect Natalie Gall describes her two-year office experience before changing school and returning for Part 2. 'My first year out was probably an average Part 1 experience of working on planning applications and presentation documents. My second year out as a Part 1, however, was completely different. In a review with my director, I asked for construction experience to expand my learning – and, amazingly, they delivered. A month later, I was on a new team working on tender drawings for a five-star hotel. I got to design, draw, build and hand over the entire back

4.5
Cullinan Studio: Design Day.
Collaborative working in multi-experienced teams is a prerequisite of office life. The development of good communication skills (both drawn and verbal) enables swift problem solving as a team.

of house for the hotel, which is where I found myself excel most. I went through every RIBA work stage and got amazing client exposure, which for a Part 1, let me tell you, is an amazing opportunity. It is through this second year alone that I learned just how we build buildings.'

If you want more work that interests you, ask your office if you can be more involved in all aspects of its work. This could be attending client meetings and design team meetings, briefing consultants and working with them, or compiling specifications, dealing with planning permission forms and regulations, and going on site visits and meetings. Try to gain first-hand experience of contract management, risk registers and critical paths, cost analysis, contingency and final accounts, as well as the different consultants' roles and how they need to be coordinated. These are all skills that will be valuable in practice, and learning as much as you can at this stage will prepare you well for life after school.

While you will be a junior member of the team, you are still valuable, and can provide unique perspectives and ideas. Steve Tompkins of Haworth Tompkins describes their office and its non-hierarchical emphasis on mutual support and learning: 'Our practice works on the basis that anyone, from a Part 1 assistant to a director, can have a good idea and everyone is part of the same creative conversation. We never forget that the studio is a teaching and learning space, but that works both ways because students bring so much positive energy and fresh thinking into the mix. Part of our job is to nurture and direct that energy within a professional framework. It's encouraging that the vast majority of our assistants have wanted to return to us full-time after graduating.'

To enhance your own professional focus, it's valuable to reflect on the nature of the practice(s) you work in: How do they get work? How do they resource their office? What are the team dynamics like? What is the management structure? How much time do they spend on competitions? If the staff turnover is high, why? What sort of fee bids are submitted? How are they calculated? How are pitch presentations conducted, and what language is used? It will be different from what you have learned at architecture school, and it is valuable preparation for your career post-university.

Another thing to remember is that you will be returning to school, which means your intellectual curiosity must be sustained and your design dexterity exercised. If you have time, consider entering architectural competitions.

You can enter competitions alone or with friends, and try to keep visiting buildings and reading architectural books, honing your intellectual ambitions and preoccupations. Extra work will show a commitment to architectural study and will help with your interview for a Part 2 course. You can find competitions from a variety of sources: design magazines, the RIBA, international competitions, local councils. They vary from relatively

4.6
Haworth Tomkins Architects.
Sketching is still an important skill for an architect. Even in the age of the computer rendering, sketching is a crucial way to develop ideas quickly.

4.7
Haworth Tomkins Architects, design review presentation.
It is common to have presentations of current work in the office and to invite comments from non-team members of the office.

quick, small-ideas competitions such as a pavilion design, to more complicated building or urban design proposals. To enter competitions and work in an office requires considerable time management skills, but it can be hugely worthwhile in building your experience and confidence.

COMMUNITY

Adapting to a new workplace and unfamiliar people can be slightly disorienting at first. There is a lot of work to be done in offices, with staff conducting themselves professionally and getting their tasks completed, while contributing to the team effort and meeting deadlines.

As well as working, it's always valuable to be a proactive participant in office life. Architect and partner of Cullinan Studio Hannah Durham describes their office attitude to year-out students and the office social life: 'Part 1 and Part 2 assistants are immersed in our egalitarian culture, including learning through sharing knowledge, and encouraged to fully participate in project work and office activities. Project teams have regular catch-ups, enabling assistants to understand the wider workings of a project beyond their own contributions, and are included in client and consultant meetings and site visits. As part of the office family, assistants are added to the rotas for making Friday lunch for the office, tea making, lunch chairing and lunch clearers.'

Keep a record of what you have done, and images of projects. This may have to be negotiated with the office, as some schemes and documents contain sensitive information.

4.8
Cullinan Studio Friday Lunch.
Offices often have rich social lives. This office makes time for an all-office Friday lunch with invited external guests. The office members take it in turns to prepare food.

Preparing to return to university and picking your route

Think ahead about your return to academia and Part 2, and apply early if possible. In the UK, there is an emerging series of different routes to Part 2, and these are set to become even more varied in the near future. Two examples are the University of Cambridge Part 2-validated Master of Philosophy in Architecture and Urban Design, and the London School of Architecture's Professional Diploma in Designing Architecture. Cambridge's method requires each candidate to apply with a well thought-out research proposal. Student work is conducted over the course of 22 months, including a six-month fieldwork period, which is used to assemble a strong body of primary and secondary research for the written MPhil. During the MArch years, students produce a resolved design proposal supported by drawings and models, as well as a 15,000-word research thesis on a topic that is symbiotic with their design work. At the LSA, students in their first year are employed for three days a week in an office for 12 months. The rest of the time they work on LSA projects and, in their second year, they are at the LSA full-time.

Similar to its Part 1 offer, an alternative route to Part 2 can be pursued with Oxford Brookes University's RIBA Studio. Director Dr Maria Faraone explains: 'RIBA Studio is a unique and flexible route to qualification for the RIBA Diploma, only for people working full-time under the supervision of an architect in the European Economic Area (EEA), Isle of Man, Channel Islands or Switzerland. The diploma courses leads to equivalent awards with respect to Part 2. Students, although predominantly UK based, are located throughout the EEA and the Channel Islands. This is an inclusive and independent study course for students who would like to direct their approach to architectural education according to a timeline and with foci of interest that are important to them.'

AVAILABLE ROUTES AND STUDENT PERCEPTIONS
Mathew Margetts, Lecturer at Newcastle University

There is now a potentially bewildering array of 'alternative courses' available for Part 2 graduates, and it is not always easy to compare their relative merits. Many of the courses are new, or comparatively recent (with the notable exceptions of Bath and Cardiff). Options range from full-time apprenticeship models that are office based, through hybrid collaborative practice routes (one year in practice, one year at university) to sandwich courses with practice-based modules.

From discussions with students as part of the RIBA North East Education Group, a picture is emerging that students have a range of reasons for choosing alternative courses, and sometimes these are not always fully informed decisions. The sense is that Part 2 graduates are not necessarily choosing alternative courses to save money (as they are increasingly speculating that student debts beyond Part 1 will effectively never be paid back), but that choices are often based on enjoying office culture more than university. Universally, however, it was noted that juggling 'work' and education is not the easy option, and requires a practice sympathetic to the peaks and troughs of academic course demands.

RIBA Studio student Wenwen Wang balanced qualification with a job at Foster + Partners, working on landmark projects and being a young mother: 'The route of obtaining an architecture qualification through this office-based programme is challenging when balancing work and family life, but with flexibility in course structure, careful planning, a bit stronger determination and self-discipline, it is definitely achievable, and the opportunity for self-learning and improvement should be cherished.'

Another possible route at master's level is an apprenticeship. Apprentices work in offices and draw salaries, but do not pay fees and are allocated 20% of their time to attend school, which allows for completion of Part 2 over a longer period of three or four years. Apprenticeships are typically mapped through to RIBA qualification within existing Part 2 courses to achieve accreditation. At Part 2, there is currently more choice and more ways to study than at Part 1 – South Bank University, Northumbria University, De Montfort University, Oxford Brookes, University of West England, Nottingham University and Cambridge University, among others, are all possibilities for those wanting to follow this route.

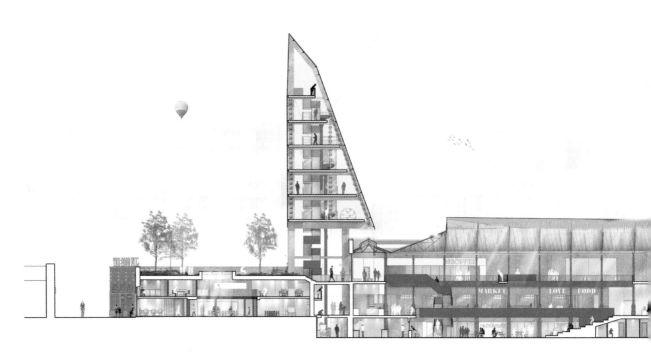

CHOOSING THE RIGHT SCHOOL FOR PART 2

The decision for many will be straightforward – perhaps you are going back to your old school because you were successful there before, most of your architectural friends are going back and you have experienced the ethos of the school and the tutors.

However, others decide to widen their network by moving to a school in a larger city (e.g. London, Manchester, Liverpool), a campus-based school or simply a school with a higher reputation. It's important to remember that there isn't a 'right' decision, and much depends on your own personal preference.

If you're reviewing league tables published by magazines or newspapers, keep in mind that they don't necessarily consider subjective preferences, and that different schools have particular specialisms. Use these league tables intelligently in conjunction with other ways of assessing schools, such as looking at the RIBA President's Medals and other prizes. Unlike Part 1, where you apply through UCAS, Part 2 applications should be sent directly to each school you are interested in. However, much of the other advice given in this book concerning the selection of schools for Part 1 is also relevant for Part 2.

You will also have the option to study abroad. If you are pursuing this option, gather as much information as you can about how and what you will be taught, as this can vary considerably throughout the world. For example, schools in the United States often use a studio system based on a 15-week semester before moving to a new tutor and a new brief, which can affect the intellectual and design depth of projects. In other areas of the world, architectural engineering is seen as the dominant discipline. Try also to be aware of what recognition your overseas master's will have in the countries you want to ultimately practise in, and whether it has RIBA recognition, for example. See Chapter 6 for more on studying abroad.

4.9, 4.10
Paul Leonard, final project for RIBA Studio Diploma (Part 2), Dublin Food Hub: Food Security in the 21st Century. This project proposes a new food hub in Dublin with the underlying ethos of the non-profit organisation Foodcloud at its core: provision of food security. Revitalising a dilapidated Georgian market building in central Dublin, a new Foodcloud office headquarters, together with marketplace, food co-work facility and vertical farm is proposed.

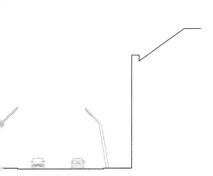

Part 2 course options
David Gloster, Director of Education, RIBA

The choice of courses a postgraduate architecture student faces has arguably never been greater. This is due not just to greater numbers of recognised schools of architecture (now more than 50 in the UK), but to a welcome growth in the confidence of those schools to define their separate identities and resist homogenisation. While those courses all reflect thresholds established by RIBA validation, schools increasingly interpret the validation criteria in creative ways to operate within diverse cultural, intellectual and professional parameters. This means that a bachelor architecture graduate must carefully review the Part 2 offer made by those schools and, very importantly, speculate on the kind of architect they wish to become; it is postgraduate study which defines the ability for critical thinking required of the properly progressive practitioner. Critical thinking enables the individual to discriminately synthesise information into knowledge.

This variety in courses reflects the pluralism offered by the studio system. Almost universal in adoption, the design studio is led by tutors promoting a particular attitude to architecture, and approach to design methodology. This allows students to follow themes they relate to and feel affection for, providing a platform from which they build their intellectual curiosity and skills. This challenges the Part 1 graduate to reflect on and articulate their own values when choosing what and where to study at Part 2.

A second, increasingly potent, influence is the growth of practice-complemented learning, and the straddling by students while they study both the world of work and an enquiring academic environment. There have been practice-based courses available at Part 2 for some time in schools as diverse as Sheffield Hallam, Cambridge, the London School of Architecture, and the distance-learning programme offered by the RIBA, RIBA Studio. These allow a student to retain a position in practice, but simultaneously progress to a postgraduate degree (university tuition fees still apply to these courses).

However, opportunities for workplace-based learning have recently been enhanced by the introduction of architecture apprenticeships; these reflect a (rather exaggerated) view from some sectors of the profession that perceived rifts between academia and practice need healing. As of September 2019, an apprenticeship can be followed at London South Bank University (undergraduate and postgraduate levels), De Montfort University and the University of the West of England (both postgraduate only). Many more apprenticeships are likely to be offered in the near future, all at Part 2: Northumbria, Oxford Brookes, Cambridge, Portsmouth, Nottingham Trent and Sheffield Hallam have all expressed an intention to offer postgraduate apprenticeships within the next year or two. An apprenticeship allows the individual to work and study at the same time – but without the burden of tuition fees.

Sensibly, a note of caution should be sounded; it was the retreat from articling between the late 1920s and late 1950s that saw architectural education entrusted to the universities, and removed from the drawing office. In Sir Leslie Martin's conclusions to the 1958 Oxford Conference on architectural education, he suggested that the workplace lacked capacity and appetite for research, and could not provide the intellectual roughage required for postgraduate study. While some modern practice now contradicts this view, the Part 1 graduate has to consider what their interest is in testing the boundaries of architecture (at perhaps the Architectural Association, or the Bartlett), or whether they subscribe to a more traditional view of the discipline. It might be concluded then that the real choice a Part 2 student makes is between progressive or normative architecture, i.e. a desire to define their own professional path, or engage with the heartland of practice.

The reality is more nuanced than that. Studios range from loosely defined aggregations of self-determining individuals (e.g. Barbara Goldstein's Co-op unit at the AA in the 1970s) to scary groups of zealots closely imitative of a methodological or tectonic orthodoxy. Technology for some may be regarded as a driver (such as the Technical Studies in Architecture group at Loughborough University), or for others as a means to an end – and, quite possibly, regarded as someone else's responsibility. Theories and histories of architecture can be seen as fundamental to authentic design – or too semantically dense to inform fine architecture. Similarly, professional skills are either wholly limited to the outhouse of Part 3 – or introduced early in the programme as fundamental, to support understanding of the context in which architecture is financed, conceived and delivered. The experience of being taught within any subject- or pedagogy-specific studio is that it places emphasis on key ideological and practical priorities, while demoting consideration of others. Some students enjoy this; others crave a more general account of the issues in architecture. Only critical reflection and self-knowledge can help the Part 1 graduate reach optimum conclusions when probing the Part 2 offer.

And no school will, or should, stand up to say it's wholly driven by design methodologies – or by technology, theory or professional values. Narrow definitions must be avoided. The breadth of Part 2 architectural education is then very complex; the Part 1 graduate must make their decisions about courses using instinct, intuition, insider knowledge and first-hand impressions of the schools they're considering. Only this rigorous and time-consuming approach will ensure their postgraduate study reflects who they are – and what they want to be. Once made, though, the correct choice is life-affirming, and life-changing.

PREPARING YOUR APPLICATION

Re-applying means you will have to prepare a new portfolio. This is another opportunity to showcase that you are architecturally creative, enthusiastic and ambitious, and display that you have developed as a student.

The portfolio should be produced in chronological order because the interviewer will want to see a sustained architectural development over the previous few years. Consider using your last and best second-year project (although it should be used as a starter), your good third-year project work, year-out work and, finally, any competition or self-instigated work. The year-out work should demonstrate a progression from your degree design work and will showcase some of the new skills you have learned while away from university. Try to show only your most interesting office work rather than everything.

When talking about each project, rehearse what you are going to say and include the reasons why you have included it in your portfolio. These might include how you have dealt with a complex brief, a complex site and a difficult set of details, or how you have utilised complex analogue or digital techniques.

INTERVIEW TIPS FOR PART 2

1. Aim to demonstrate that you have the skills and aptitude for postgraduate study.
2. Avoid over-elaborating to the point that you run out of interview time.
3. Self-evaluate, and think critically about your own work. Consider how you might have done your third-year project differently based on the experience you now have.
4. Prepare a few questions about the course and the way it operates, future employability and the ethos of the school (even if you believe you secretly know the answers).

If you have multiple offers, decide which schools best suit you and the sort of architect you have ambitions to be. Accept an offer and re-focus on your year-out work. Once you have decided where you are going, keep an eye on the school, ask for the current student handbook and start to read some of the reading lists.

The cost of Part 2 courses and the relative modes of study may also influence your decision. Part 2 must be undertaken no more than three academic years after completing Part 1 in order for you to be considered as a continuing student and remain on the same student finance package. Students who plan to complete Part 2 on a part-time basis having studied Part 1 full-time are not considered as being on a single course, and are therefore not entitled to apply for tuition fee or maintenance loans for their Part 2 studies. However, students may be eligible for a Postgraduate Loan where they are ineligible for undergraduate support.

To prepare for Part 2 study, it's worth visiting your school's end-of-year show in the summer before you join to study recent work, absorb the show catalogue and gain insight into where the school is at that precise moment.

Five ways to get ahead

1. Apply early.
2. Prepare your office interview portfolio.
3. Once in a job, start registering your experience on the PEDR.
4. Be a proactive member of the office team.
5. Research schools to return to study at when your year out comes to an end.

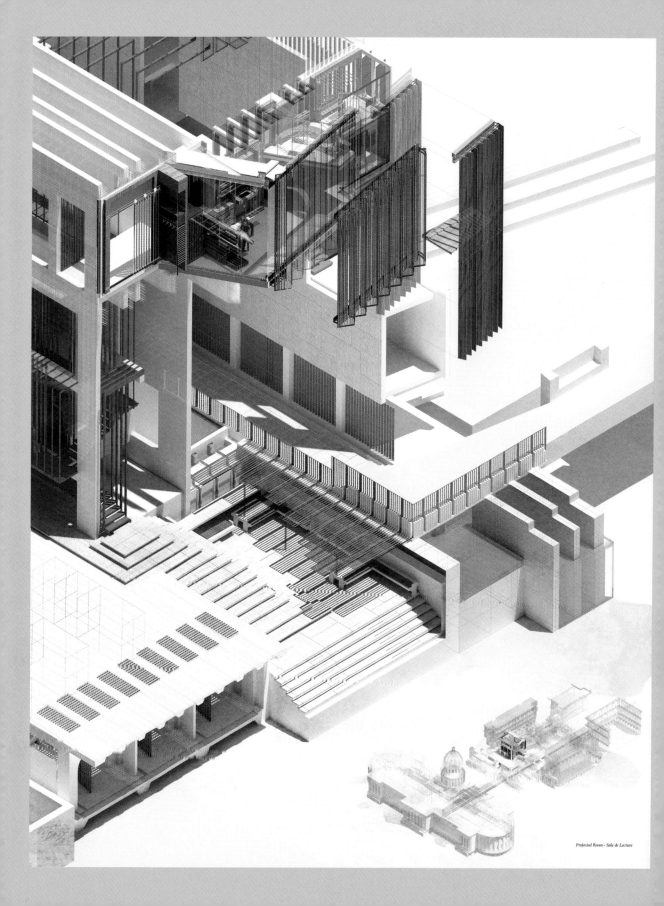

Projected Room - Sala de Lectura

MArch and Part 2

Starting your master's in architecture (Part 2)

Part 2 architectural education gives you the opportunity to consolidate what you have learned at undergraduate level and the experiences and lessons you have had in your year(s) out. This consolidation and the added complexity of briefs, sites, experimentation and intellectual engagement will be a two-year (or three-year, if part-time) journey culminating in the final projects of your academic architectural design education, where you can really show off your design and technical talents.

This work is often accompanied by a lengthy written thesis. During these years, you will transform from an undergraduate with a level of 'awareness' of architectural concepts, construction, professionalism and ambition to a fledgling but capable architectural designer with a more complex knowledge of all the parameters that the architectural profession deals with. Your subsequent Part 3 experience and case studies will further elucidate this knowledge in terms of contract law, project administration and professionalism. Students can really bloom in these final years at school, developing a new confidence and a proactive, experimental, yet technically proficient architectural persona – and develop eminently employable skills, too.

All Part 2 students should demonstrate skills and knowledge aligned with ARB's General Criteria. The key difference between Part 1 and Part 2 study is the ability to demonstrate complex architectural and urban problem solving, often with new ideas, hypotheses and speculation. You will start to apply disparate sources of knowledge such as history, theory, materiality, detailing and environmental concerns with ambition and research, coupled with the ability to appraise and test your speculations and be critical about them.

This self-critical appraisal will fuel further, better iterations of your work, which you will begin to present with increasing familiarity with appropriate media. You will notice your written work improve, as you become equally well argued and researched, with a balance between design and written work. You will also learn how to make professional architectural decisions in unpredictable circumstances in line with the architect's role(s) in the construction industry and its contractual manifestations. The step-up requires you to be practical enough to realise your designs in pragmatic ways – but experimental and speculative ways too.

5.1
University of Edinburgh, Jessica Barton, La Casa de las Personas, Year 5. **The MArch demands a fuller understanding of building tectonics. Here the building is represented as a series of layers and wraparounds of different materials, with different opacities.**

5.2
Bartlett, University College London,
Tasnim Eshraqi Najafabadi, Radical
Regionalism: A New Inter-Tidal Habitat,
Year 4.
**You may start to develop architectures
for sites that are less conventional
and explore a natural dynamic
landscape of ebbs and flows.
MArch is often about designing for
complex ecological conditions.**

For those who do a master's, it often provokes some of the best work you
will do and marks a critical stage in your architectural development. It can
be a proving ground for what might be your own distinctive way of seeing
the world and operating within it. In short, it will help you develop your
architectural vocabulary – a recognisable language in practice.

Recently qualified architect Natalie Gall remembers her Part 2: 'After taking
the two years out in industry, I was far more informed and could apply my
actual construction experience to my coursework ... In my opinion, Part 2
was far more interesting to me than Part 1, as we satisfied most of the RIBA
criteria for the course in our first year, leaving [me] the freedom to fully
speculate in [my] second year (it didn't have to be a building). My drawings
therefore became bigger and more lyrical, and I subsequently left with the
Merit for Outstanding Achievement award'.

Your relationship with your tutors at Part 2 typically matures. Discovery and development of techniques and concepts are built though discussion, discourse and conversation – known as the elenctic method. John Bell, recent leader of the Part 2 course at UCA: Canterbury describes the difference: 'The BA course necessarily covers core skills and introduces the student to design research and the representational and conceptual frameworks which attend it. The MArch is predicated on the development of critical design thinking through the elenctic method.'

At postgraduate level, the onus is on you to determine things, and tutors fulfil the role of sounding boards, whereby you can take what advice you need from them, but you are now the captain of the ship. Try to have the design in mind, focus on the architectural problem at hand and work on it as swiftly as possible.

The full spectrum of tools and methodologies developed during Part 1 and the year out can be utilised to speculate on what you might be able to achieve in the representation of your work. You will have become more dexterous in representing your propositions, whether in diagrams, models (virtual, actual or mixed), drawings, films and animation. You may also be more particular about the main features of the architectural sites you're working with, surveying them with three-dimensional scanners, drones and other technologies, which will allow you to push the boundaries.

History, theory and futures

You will typically be reaching a level where you can be more critical and strategic about what you find interesting in history, theory and futures, and how you can link contrasting ideas intellectually and architecturally. In relation to your written work, Mark Garcia advises that 'histories, theories and futures (as much as concepts, ideas and philosophy) are an imaginative and creative practice, act, event and performance'. As well as being written, they can produce new and designed forms in themselves, developing a seamless philosophical agenda that is related to your architectural design work.

At the Architectural Association, Mark Morris describes how they encourage a synergy between design and history theory and futures: 'MArch students have a wide choice of history and theory seminars. These do not necessarily align with specific unit briefs, but the spectrum of topics and research methods embraced by these advanced seminars lets MArch students find a pathway that links up to many studio preoccupations. Students may elect to do a written thesis as an extension of the fifth-year studio project and such writing is supported by history and theory studies tutors.'

At Part 1 level, history and theory are taught most often as 'survey' courses that make the student aware of the foundational concepts, whereas at Part 2 the student is expected to deploy this accumulated knowledge in the service of a researched, structured and logical argument that explores wider interests.

It's valuable to speak to your tutors and be aware of exactly what you are being asked to do and the level at which you are being asked to do it. This allows you to be in control of your architectural education and manage deadlines and expectations in a conscientious way. You should prepare for each crit, essay and brief in advance, and use the summer between fourth and fifth year to prepare and gather information for your 'thesis' year.

5.3
University of Greenwich, David Pow, Bioluminous Architectural Compositions, Year 5.

5.4
University of Greenwich, William Bryan, The Bridge of Guilds, Year 5.
You should in your master's be approaching a total synthesis between your design work and your written work. This project was a seamless synthesis between theory, technology and design.

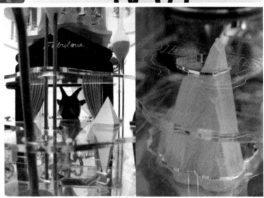

5.5
University of Brighton, Imran Sammee,
Prosthetic Hedgerow, Year 4.
A master's can be about exploring new building typologies and developing hybrid briefs and programmes, bringing one way of thinking into contact with another.

Realising architecture

SKILLS

The ARB criteria for Part 2 are fairly stringent, and demand knowledge of, and the ability to deploy, a wide range of facts, protocols, understandings, histories, theories and technologies in architecture. Part 2 is both an opportunity to explore architecture as the science of where it is as a profession now, and to speculate on the future of architecture. Different schools do this differently; some let fourth years deal with more pragmatic ideas and leave speculation to fifth years, while others map the ARB criteria for Part 2 across the two years full-time, or three years part-time, in a variety of ways.

There is no standard structure for the number and timing of projects – it will depend on the school. You will typically receive a brief, a client and a site/geographical region at first, or you may be allowed to pick your own combination of the first two to meet your intellectual and architectural preoccupations. Sites are commonly tied in with an international field trip.

5.6
University of Coventry, Rebecca Bubb,
AL[AM]MANAC, Year 4.
Some students initially like to work with annotated diagrams to gain an understanding of the scope of the brief and the programme. Diagramming and its associated theorising has a long history in architecture.

AL[AM]MANAC

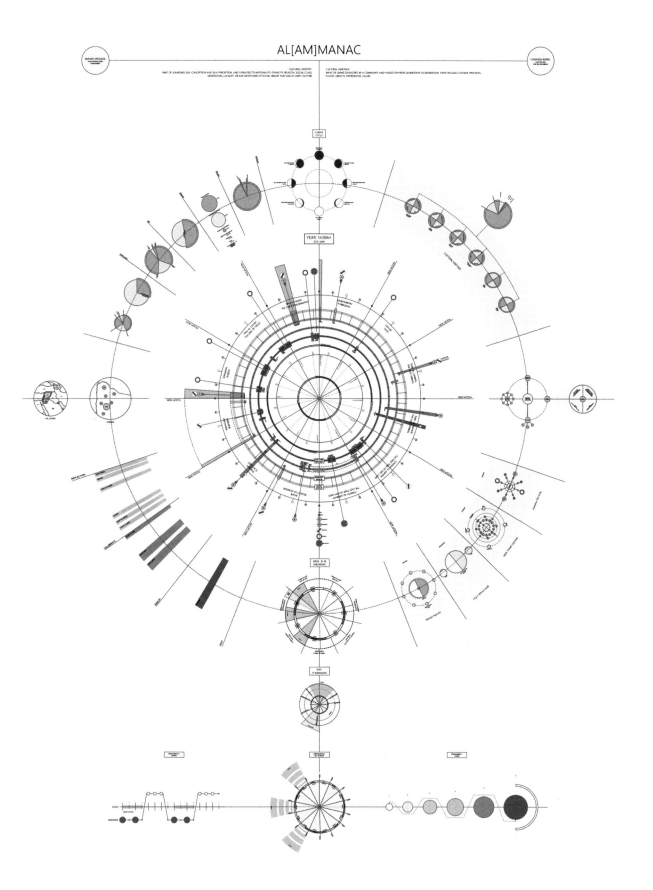

Students will be asked to develop a full understanding of the site in terms of its actual materiality and its history, as well as its urban/rural/suburban configuration in its wider context. Diligent site analysis provides historical and material understanding of a site and its context. It is also necessary to understand the legislative context of a site and the restrictions that this imposes. A site may be subject to a plethora of covenants, tree preservation orders, mixed ownership, council urban development plans, conservation areas, listed buildings and planning regulations. These will determine what you will be able to achieve in your design.

You might need to find a client or a group of clients, and your brief-writing abilities will be tested; you could be asked to speculate on where the funding for your building might come from and the dynamic of a mix of funders, some private and some public.

RIBA PLAN OF WORK

The RIBA Plan of Work and its supporting documentation (see Appendix 2) is an important schedule of the architect's work stages. It is also crucial in how your experience is mapped in your PEDR, and you will be familiar with it from your year out. The RIBA Plan of Work matrix cross-references key design team tasks such as costing, risk assessment and town planning applications against seven key work stages: Strategic Definition, Preparation and Brief, Concept Design, Developed Design, Construction, Handover and Close Out, and In Use. Familiarity with this document will be useful when considering and designing more complex buildings.

Every decision you make as a designer has cost implications. As you progress through the seven stages of the RIBA Plan of Work, the costing becomes increasingly predictable. Each stage of the Plan of Work requires a sustainability check, and you should think about how construction materials are procured and delivered in this respect.

PROFESSIONAL AND LEGAL FRAMEWORKS

You will be asked at some point to demonstrate your understanding of the professional, managerial and legal frameworks, as well as the teams you will need to form and work within. Consider if it will be suitable for a design and build contract, or a more traditional contract, or something else?

The nature of the contract will influence the type and duration of various consultants appointed (and their responsibilities), and the changing relationship of the architect to the contractor, their subcontractors and the client as the design and construction progresses. It's important to weigh up the pros and cons of each contractual arrangement and the relationship of cost, quality and time, and consider how you will staff your project team from your notional office at particular points of the commission.

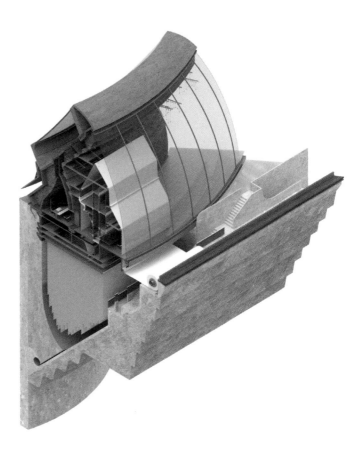

5.7
University of Brighton, Edward Crump,
The Architectural Algorithm, Year 5.
MArch will also require the ability
of a student to conceive and draw
complex details, where multiple
materials come together.

Reconciling these parameters and achieving a high-quality design is a large part of your task. Initially, you will be asked to produce a sketch proposal that starts to delineate a solution to these issues. This will help you produce the first sketch scheme quickly, trying to design elements of the building that are multivalent, i.e. those that have more than one beneficial effect on the building. Design with a purity of concept – it will add intellectual weight to what you are doing. It will also order the emphasis of parts of a building within a design.

In preparing for real-life work as an architect, it's also necessary to understand critical paths and risk registers. The critical path affects the overall time delivery/phasing of a building, and the procurement of materials and their installation, and every building has a critical path peculiar to itself. A Gantt chart can be drawn that shows what elements

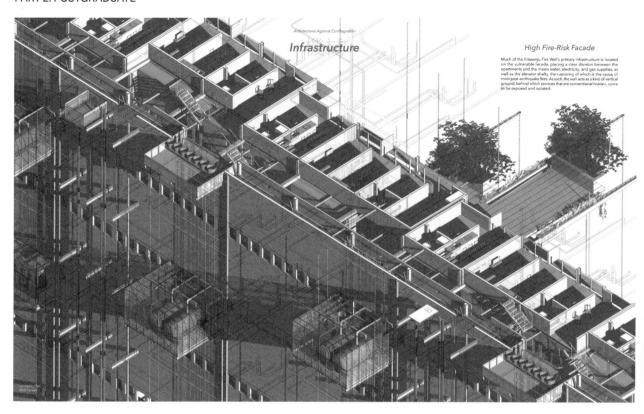

Architecture Against Conflagration

Infrastructure

High Fire-Risk Facade

Much of the Kitasenju Fire Wall's primary infrastructure is located on the vulnerable facade, placing a clear division between the apartments and the mains water, electricity, and gas supplies, as well as the elevator shafts, the rupturing of which is the cause of most post-earthquake fires. As such, the wall acts as a kind of vertical ground, behind which services that are conventional hidden, come to be exposed and isolated.

5.8
University of Edinburgh,
Christopher McCallum, Rishabh Shah
and Callum Rowland, Carp Dragon
Snake Dance.
**MArch will require the student to
design their work in respect of building
regulations and to communicate these
strategies efficiently.**

5.9
Mackintosh School of Architecture,
Eugenio Cappuccio, The Culinary
Cathedral, Year 4.
**MArch is also about the ambiance
and atmosphere you can create as an
architect; sometimes these can be
calming and contemplative, sometimes
a little more dynamic.**

of the building need to be started or completed before others can begin. For example, floor finishes can't be laid before the screed is done, while second-fix electrics cannot be done before the first fix. You can only tile a bathroom after it has been plumbed in. Not all elements of the building are on the critical path, but the primary elements are included.

You will usually be asked to present all this information in report form. If you produce it well, it is the sort of document that will give you a very good chance of being offered a post-Part 2 job because it shows you have the range of knowledge and skills useful to an office. The report should be clear and not overly wordy – preferably presenting an idea in a diagram. You will be required to develop a generic base of different types of diagram. For example, an axonometric can be used and reused, marked up and doctored to show structure, duct runs and service risers, etc. Bubble diagrams can help to show the connections and interaction between spaces, or arrowed circulation paths through your building, and sectional cuts and plan diagrams that show air circulation.

5.10
University of East London,
Boon Wei Phum, Year 5.
The axonometric can be deployed in many situations to show a variety of spatial, material and constructional arrangements.

Together with these pragmatic concerns, you will also be asked to speculate on the nature of architecture and its future. When, where and for how long depends on a particular school's course/module design, and is often supported by the history and theory dissertation or written thesis.

Looking to the future: architectural speculation

Changes in technology have manifested themselves in many ways – how we procure, fund, design and make buildings. Architecture doesn't stop with buildings: it encompasses cities, landscapes and environments (all have virtual and actual components). Materials are changing, and the pre-eminence of hard and dry materials is being challenged by soft and wet materiality. Top-down construction methods are being questioned by emergent bottom-up paradigms.

Where does all this place architectural schools within this miasma of change? Arguably, right at the centre of the vortex, riding the surf on a continuing precarious but exhilarating trajectory. The schools are absolutely crucial to the research, development and continued evolution of agile, decent, and dynamic and connected environments, which makes them special and valuable.

5.11
University of Strathclyde, Law Yik Yung,
The Fun Complex, Year 4.
Students at master's level should
be encouraged to be bold and
confident and to try ways to make their
architecture contemporary and original.

Today, it's incredibly difficult to escape the digital world's embraces and frustrations. As designers and human beings, we flit between the real, augmented and virtual thousands of times a day. Our cones of vision have multiplied a thousand times in the last half-century, and the seemingly absurd protocols of Surrealism seem more appropriate than the clean restraint of Modernism in this fecund technological era. The one thing that is crucial for architectural schools to teach is mental and spatial dexterity, way above the tired supposed dynamism of clean lines, pure boxes, glass walls and order. We live in a world where your duvet can blog, you can print a fork with your desktop 3D printer, and you can create an augmented reality storm. All of these, and many more spatial opportunities and conditions, are architectural.

Some might ask, do all architecture students need to be proficient with all these technologies? Won't there be specialisms? However, it's possible you won't be able to function as an architect soon without them, and that

5.12
University of Greenwich, William Bryan,
The Bridge of Guilds, Year 5.
It is important for postgraduate
students to experiment with
the formal and intellectual
content of their architecture.

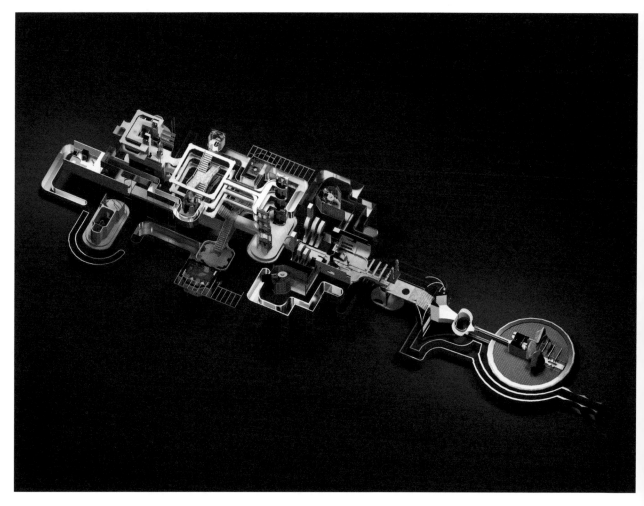

5.13
University of Greenwich, Marilia Lezou,
Hotel Mollino, Year 5.
**Students should use MArch to
further their understanding of their
architectural preoccupations. This
student had an interest in Carlo Mollino,
and developed a hotel using some of his
architectural tropes.**

5.14
Royal College of Art, Christopher Sejer
Fischlein, Fundamental Rite II;
Rectum Set, Year 5.
**Students are encouraged to experiment
across media, crossing the digital/real
divide many times in a project. Different
technologies of representation have
different strengths and weaknesses.**

such ideas, spatial reflexivity and concepts are the new telephone, set square, drawing board and construction techniques of the architect's trade.

Being an architecture student in a post-digital world

You are an architecture student in the 'post-digital' world. Within the context of Part 2, this fact will impact on the architectural designs and scenarios you need to develop much more than during Part 1. Some schools, studios and units don't explore virtual technologies in great detail; however, all students exist and are educated within a technological context.

First, it is important to stress that 'post-digital architecture' is not an architecture without any digital component. Indeed, it is an architecture that is very much a synthesis between the virtual, actual, biological, augmented and mixed. It is impossible to talk of digital architecture as a binary opposition to normal real-world architecture when virtuality has insinuated itself into our existence at every scale and at every turn.

Schools are taking these matters seriously and looking to the future. As MArch Design Coordinator Mike Aling at Greenwich University observes: 'MArch is a testing ground for initiating future forms of practice, and allows students to operate as generalists and specialists simultaneously. The increasingly rich overlaps between architecture and emerging technologies such as AR, AI and Big Data are interrogated to their fullest. Successful MArch courses should allow students to speculate on how to answer the hard problems of the future.'

John Bell, recently at UCA, describes its approach to evolving technology and student options: 'We support working in building information management and virtual reality with specialist seminars and workshops – in the MArch students can elect to take a studio which has a more explicitly technologically driven agenda.'

When an architect designs, they make space by putting things together, creating void from mass and mass from void. When you put things together, it's good if they can do more than one job – to be multivalent. An element can be structural, or decorated, or change in position related to a predetermined algorithm, and the algorithm might be able to fluctuate in time, changing its criteria and optimisation logistics. Narratives can be constructed about the whole or the parts that allow you to develop deeper and more resonantly complex semiotics.

Every architectural designer is different and feels that they have something original to bring to the world, solving a problem in an original or idiosyncratic way. No two designers are the same, no two designs the same, no two sites are the same, and no two observers or users are the same (and all change over time and have varying durations). These facts

5.15
Bartlett, University College London,
Sonia Magdziarz, How to Carve a Giant,
Year 5.
**The master's is a chance to think of
architecture in its broadest terms,
in strange terrains and in
atmospheric situations.**

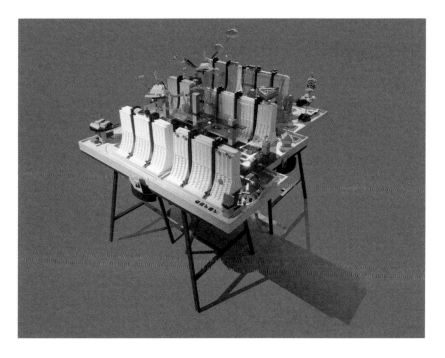

5.16
University of Greenwich, James Lawton,
Alt-Erlaa-Gamified, Year 5.
**An interest in virtual 'world' building
can also be encouraged with the use
of gaming engines to create episodic,
algorithmic, architectural space.**

5.17
Architectural Association, Eyal
Geovannetti, A Line in the Landscape,
Year 5.
The brief focused on urban
archaeology, drawing machines and
atmospheres. Unveiling the presence
and absence of the city's past. The slow
gathering of architectural fragments
forms the depths of an immeasurable
archive; one that manifests itself
physically in the city through spaces
of continual flux and rewriting.

5.18
London South Bank University.
Yakim Milev, Oxford Street, London Tower,
Year 5.
The ability to swiftly explore
and optimise the formal, spatial
and structural configurations of
projects can be much enhanced
with digital imaging.

should lead you to view the world as exceptional, as a series of personal and conversational mnemonic events. Your design work within this blooming tapestry should do nothing more than exploit this paradigm.

The experience of contemporary architectural designers is one of positioning their work in relation to seven spectrums:

1. **Space:** There is a continuum of architectural space that stretches from having no computer, mobile phone, connectivity or digital presence whatsoever to full bodily immersion in virtual reality. Along the way between these two extremes are all manner of mixed and augmented spaces.

2. **Technology:** Ranging from simple prosthetics (the stone axe) via the Victorian cog and cam, to the valve, capacitor, logic gate, integrated circuit, central processing unit, quantum computer, stem cell, nanobot and a million states and applications between and beyond.

3. **Narrative, semiotics and performance:** An architect or designer can choose whether their work operates along a continuum that ranges from minimal engagement in quotation or mnemonic nuance in relation to the history of culture, to full-blown historical quotation and evoking the memories of a past age or period/style in architecture. A design might conjure new conjunctions of semiotics as a way of re-reading them. It can also integrate itself with human and cultural memory reflexively or performatively (in real time or retrospectively).

4. **Cyborgian geography:** An architect can posit work which operates in all manner of mixed and augmented terrains that are subject to all manner of geo-locative, geomorphic and cybermorphic factors and drivers.

5. **Scopic regimes:** Architecture can exist at all scales. It all depends on the resolution of the scope that one chooses to use – continents, oceans, cities, streets, rooms, carpets, micro-landscapes and medico-landscapes are all on this continuum.

6. **Sensitivity:** A designer might decide to make objects, spaces or buildings whose parts are sensitive and pick up environmental variations or receive information. Sensors can make objects and buildings that are influenced by events elsewhere or indeed are influential elsewhere. Sometimes, though, it might be preferable to make 'dumb' objects instead of 'smart' objects and architectures.

7. **Time:** The most important of these continua. All the above six continua can be time-dependent. Therefore, designers can 'mix' the movement of their spaces, buildings and objects up and down the other six continua. A design can oscillate the spaces within itself with varying elements of virtuality/sensitivity over time, using different technologies

5.19
University of Strathclyde, Evangelia Giannoulaki and Marina Konstantopoulou, Synchroni[CITY] 1 and 2, Year 5.
The master's can also be an opportunity to think at a wider urban infrastructural level, making architectural interventions within the wider networks of the city.

5.20
Mackintosh School of Architecture,
James Dalley, The Misinformation
Ecosystem, Year 5.
**Sometimes students may work
polemically and allegorically,
addressing aspects of current
discussion like 'fake news'
or propaganda.**

5.21, 5.22
Royal College of Art, Livia Wang,
A Guided Tour, Year 5.
**A good student will explore all manner
of ways to communicate their spatial
desires and dexterity. This can be
installation art, virtual and actual
modelling, drawing, and sometimes
immersing the viewer in the virtual.**

at different times in its existence. It's also possible to perform complex mnemonic tableaux at certain points in its life cycle, or demand of its occupants the use of different lenses with which to see other than anthropocentric phenomena or spaces. A design might coerce the occupant to be aware of environmental conditions in other locations that change, or change the sensitivity of objects over time, dulling them sometimes, making them hypersensitive at other times.

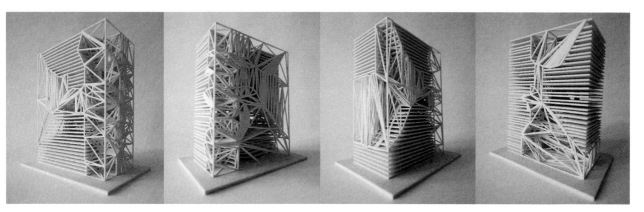

5.23
London South Bank University, Selvei Al-Assadi, Structural Matrices Studies, Year 5.
Students can create numerous versions of virtual and 3D-printed models and prototypes to explore structural systems for buildings.

In other words, it is the negotiation and understanding of these continua that will give us the opportunity mentally, physically and virtually to create post-digital architectures. While the descriptions of the continua are necessarily relatively simple, the manifestations of post-digital architecture are extraordinary and infinite.

It's worth noting that we don't include sustainable criteria in these continua, and this is for two reasons: first, any design work done in the 21st century must be sustainable and, second, sustainability should be embedded in all the seven continua – they cannot exist without issues of sustainability and indeed ethics.

For millennia, the simple act of building has been one of destruction – or at the very least, ecological truncation and rearticulating. Things and relationships are lost while others are formed. A post-digital architecture needs to buck the entropic trend and be smart enough to comprehend and, if required, respond to the myriad natural and artificial ecologies within which it sits. Architecture should be bedded into a landscape of ecology that far exceeds the boundaries of any specific site, country or continent, and it is the spatial manipulation of the relationships in these ecologies in which their architecture resides. Architects must understand, appreciate and design within the natural imperative of flora, fauna, machines and networks, and be capable of husbanding the forces of biochemistry, virtuality, movement patterns, the seasonal and diurnal, and even millennial perturbations, and accommodate and rearticulate slow and abrupt phase changes of sites and landscapes.

The architecture of augmented reality

5.24
University of Greenwich, Liam Bedwell,
The Lithium Empire, Year 5.
**Sometimes students will create
'process' buildings. This design for a
factory explores lithium production
for batteries.**

Some Part 2 students are now embedding augmented reality (AR)
scenarios within their architectural propositions. AR begins at the initial
conceptual stage of a design when a student decides to give a user not
only a real-world spatial experience, but also a virtual one. The next design
decisions are when and how the two or multiple worlds interact, how the
AR will be seen, and for how long. AR will radically shift how architects
conceive, represent and build architecture. Architecture will be a spatial
dance between virtual spaces and actual spaces, slipping and sliding from
one to the other in a symbiotic relationship, with each supporting the other.
Real architecture and virtual architecture can cosset, respond and interact
to create hybrid spaces personally and individually designed and used
that are geo-located and maybe nested by millions of users in the same
location, unseen or seen by others.

5.25, 5.26
Royal College of Art, Livia Wang,
A Guided Tour, Year 5.
**Students may choose to place part
of their project in virtual, mixed
or augmented realities and create
narratives of uses and occupants.**

Digital augmented space is infinite, and is the first indication of the end
of scarcity for architectural space – it produces a ubiquity of possible
architectural interventions. The personal ability of users of architecture
to interact with its spaces and lineaments (real and virtual) is much
enhanced. Spaces can be personalised to a much greater extent due to
augmented reality. The user is an active participant, more than ever before,
and often the designer of their own augmented spaces. This is because
augmented space is individual, geo-located and, from a unique personal
point of view, like architecture itself. Its synthesis into architecture offers a
myriad of architectural possibilities.

Augmented space allows you to erase people, walls and objects.
Architects/designers of augmented architecture will use erasure as
a prime architectural tactic, and an expansion of the whole gamut of
architectural tactics and spatial protocols is imminent. Augmented objects
are without gravity or weight when you interact with them – unless their
designer wants them to have weight; the 'weight' of an augmented reality
object is an architectural design decision. In time, it will become just as
haptic, sensual and sensitive as any real-world architectural condition as
bandwidth increases.

133

The history of the architectural avant-garde, the paper architects and the techno-visionary architects, have left architects well placed for the creation of these worlds. The are no rules, dogmas or doctrines in these spaces, which will have their own rarefied spatial logics – nothing is too surreal or too hyperlinked. Nothing is spatially *verboten* and nothing is impossible, architecturally speaking, any more.

There are, of course, huge ramifications in terms of privacy, hacking, ethics, personality theft, spatial copyright, etc. The continued debates and occurrences of issues and the software inventions of cyber security provoked by this and other 'disruptive' technologies will continue apace.

The architectural uses of AI

Part 2 students are starting to use artificial intelligence (AI) and the data AI collects in their design work. Architectural assumptions about a certain client's way of operating in the world (whether individually or corporately) can be graphically represented with circulation flows, engagement with the digital media and many other aspects.

But what is AI? AI is the ability of computerised systems to make decisions utilising speech recognition, language translation, and visual perception by sifting data. There are two types of AI: 'weak' and 'strong'. Weak AI is the ability of a computer to imitate human thought, as in a computer playing chess with a human being. It seems from a human perspective that the machine is thinking, but it is simply following algorithms created and loaded on to it by human programmers. Strong AI, meanwhile, is the ability of a machine intelligence to think like a human being, which is a much more technically and ethically difficult terrain. Some believe strong AI is unattainable; however, the speed of development of computational capacity has exponentially increased, and it follows Moore's law, which states that computational capacity doubles every two years.

Where does AI mine its data? We live in a world where data is collected about all aspects of our lives and movements. We are hosts to smartphones, voice-activated virtual assistants and smart cars that collect our data and transmit it to large corporations.

What impact will it have on architects? Some of the impact of AI development is already being felt in architectural practice. Many students commonly use parametricism to help generate designs, whereby parameters for a design are algorithmically set as a series of elemental digital relationships. If one parameter is changed, the whole design changes accordingly. In a way, parametricism is weak AI – where cities and their pedestrian and vehicular flows are being analysed by AIs programmed by humans. However, it will allow architects to know their clients, sites and briefs better as it presents us with a better understanding of their preoccupations, habits, likes and dislikes by mining and evaluating their data.

5.27
Architectural Association, Ryan Cook, Cinematic Junction, Year 5.
This project, Cinematic Junction, takes a piece of redundant A13 roadway and its surroundings and repurposes it as part of a vast urban film studio intended to revitalise the site of Ford Dagenham.

5.28
University of East London, Michael On,
Civic Space and Gallery, Year 5.
It is important that students 'bed down' their architecture in ideas of community and placemaking, and are generous in the provision of civic space.

AI could accelerate the time it takes to design and build buildings, and liberate us from tedious, normative architectural tasks such as door schedules. This could happen in a variety of ways, some of which are prosaic and others extraordinary. For example, on the prosaic side, it might be able to offer fast costing alternatives or layouts, or quickly ascertain the specific intricacies of the planning regulations pertaining to a site and previous applications and sift through their salient points. On a more futuristic note, AI might be embedded in autonomous building elements that self-construct architecture or further develop smart materials.

AI can help us understand the metabolic rates of cities, how they respond to crisis and how they can be programmed to be more resilient. AI also makes the achievement of fully smart homes more likely, making our living and working spaces more responsive to our own habits and desires, as well as allowing us to see the fuel we use, the calories we consume and the exercise we take.

AI is not a threat to the creativity of the architect, and this is the most elusive part of AI for computer scientists. An architect's individual and special way of seeing and designing in the world is the most difficult thing to replicate digitally. The profession will undoubtedly change, but for architects this has always been the case. It is crucial that these 'disruptive' technologies are researched and speculated on by members of our profession, so we as architects can define the pros and cons of new technologies and not have other disciplines imposing on us their ways of seeing this emerging world. Above all it is architecture's human capital that is so vitally important to the future, and AI won't change that for the foreseeable future, if at all.

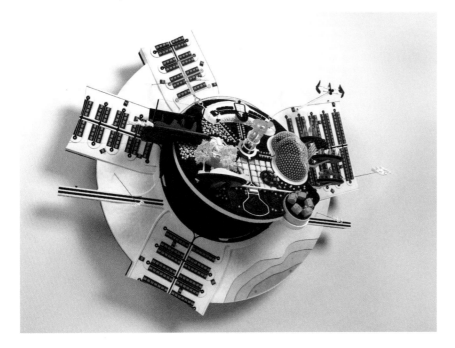

5.29
University of Greenwich, Michael Gibbs, Disney Worldbuilding, Year 5.
Architects are becoming aware that practice is changing, but their skills will still be useful. Imagination and spatial constructions are becoming increasingly important to the future.

Finishing Part 2

Part 2 will have enabled you to become more pragmatically and technically astute, as well as strengthening your ability to understand the processes and evaluation required at the various stages of a project. Furthermore, Part 2 will have given you confidence to speculate on the future of architecture, and your architectural future in all its spatial, constructional, representational, political, intellectual, contractual and sustainable guises.

Recent Part 2 graduate Ben Spong remembers: 'Fifth year felt less like an end and more like a beginning. Being given such freedom and respect with the work meant that I began to develop some notion of 'practice' – developing work that is on my own terms. In this sense, fifth year being a thesis year felt somewhat true, but it was less of a conclusion to five-plus years of architectural education and more of a provocation on my role in the future of architecture.'

Part 2 ends in assessment against the Part 2 criteria (the same subjects and skills as outlined in Part 1), involving the 'complex' knowledge and imaginative problem solving deployment of these skills and concepts. A final assessment review will likely involve a personal meeting with an external examiner, although it's worth noting that some schools do this while others discuss the marking of the student cohort with the external examiners without the students present. Meeting an external examiner to talk about your work tends to be an immensely enjoyable experience and can, sometimes, result in a job offer or interview appointment.

Five ways to get ahead

1. Keep up to date with contemporary technologies and computer packages.
2. Bring your architectural preoccupations and knowledge fully into play in your projects, both written and design.
3. Maintain your architectural ambition, don't be scared to speculate.
4. Build into your design projects notions of procurement, sustainability and construction phasing.
5. Be creative with how you present, draw and model your work; hybridise analogue and digital techniques.

141   **Studying abroad**
149   **Part 3**

Studying abroad

As an architecture student it is valuable to gain architectural experiences outside your country of residence. Students can do this at any point in their architectural education (if the school encourages it), and the processes to achieve this vary from school to school, or country to country. During the 17th and 18th century, young people of means often undertook the 'Grand Tour' to develop an understanding of Europe, its histories and its cultures, but also its art and architecture – Italy was particularly popular. Foreign field trips might be your first experience of the architectural tour, and schools often take the opportunity to set design projects abroad and use the occasion of a field trip to conduct site analysis, which can be coordinated with visits to local schools of architecture and notable buildings.

As Associate Professor Perry Kulper from the University of Michigan states: 'Architects need to be global citizens, many architects, primitive and sophisticated – feet in the mud and imaginations in the sky, simultaneously. In parallel, as architecture and its education surge toward increased global interfaces, transnational education is critical in feeding the cultural agency of architecture. On this front, the benefits of studying abroad are multiple, maybe even essential. They include: framing one's identity and own culture(s) by encountering rangy cultural values, engaging diverse ethical positions and experiencing highly varied political systems; expanding world views, and global awareness; acquiring relational versatility from working from the so-called outside; engaging broadened conceptual, strategical and tactical ranges that challenge default assumptions; and constructing increased skill range and networked affiliations. In parallel to the aforementioned global encounters, the voyager, the explorer, and the navigator must be recovered and urgently rekindled, in all of us.'

Participating in prolonged study abroad

Being in a strange city for a few days, being shown buildings you have never seen before, is fun and often unlocks creative ideas. It is another thing altogether to be domiciled in another architecture school for a few weeks, a month, a semester or even an academic year.

Most architecture schools have connections with schools in various parts of the world. These arrangements can take the form of:

- collaborations between one university and another
- foreign campuses for a home university
- a home campus for a foreign university
- arrangements for student and/or staff exchange.

6.1
Xi'an Jiaotong-Liverpool University, Suzhou, China, 'City Wanderer', Studio Project, Menghan Chen, undergraduate.
Being part of an architecture course that straddles continents and awards dual or joint degrees validated by the RIBA can be a good idea.

6.2
Xi'an Jiaotong-Liverpool University, Suzhou, China, master's studio review (photo XJLU).
It is often useful to an architect to be able to have direct experience of other cultures and ways of seeing architecture.

For example, Liverpool University also has a campus in London as well as a Chinese campus at Xi'an Jiaotong; Nottingham University has a Chinese campus at Ningbo in China.

The European Union's ERASMUS programme has facilitated many study-abroad opportunities for architecture students, to the mutual benefit of architecture schools across Europe.

The RIBA validates architecture courses across the world, with the locations of these courses expanding yearly, including Demark, Lebanon, Greece, Egypt, France, Iceland, Malaysia, Peru, Poland and South Korea. These schools go through the same arduous examination process by an RIBA Visiting Board to achieve validation, and their visiting board reports (as with all validated schools) are published on the RIBA website.

Sophie Bailey, Validation Manager at the RIBA, describes the benefits that students in RIBA-validated schools abroad have, including the 'knowledge that their academic standards are benchmarked against a rigorous, global, evidence-based system, that monitors compliance using third-party peer review by academics and construction industry practitioners. Also graduates of RIBA-recognised schools with RIBA Part 2 equivalent qualifications may become chartered members of the RIBA, with the opportunity to use the RIBA affix (in all countries except the UK).'

Before embarking on studying abroad, it is wise to consider carefully where you will go. The first simple and important consideration is whether you will be able to understand the language of tuition. Architecture has its own ways of describing material junctions, space and site, with its own shorthand and jargon, and can be difficult if tuition is not in English or a second language that you are conversant in.

Needing further consideration is pedagogy – how the subject of architecture is taught – which can vary considerably from one country to another, and can encompass several educational and cultural aspects. First, what is the relationship between staff and students – is it close? Do the professors teach, or is face-to-face teaching done by others (normally teaching assistants, or TAs)? How big is the student cohort? What is the constituency of the school – is it an Ivy League America school, a state school or a private school?

Even more detailed than your initial school selection, you'll have to consider the geographical location of the school, its history (with both the city and the country), politics and social divisions. Some schools are more technical, while others are more artistic.

Architectural education in the United Kingdom happens in a relatively liberal and consistent way, but this might not be the case in other countries. For example, the German architectural school system has four types of universities – art academies, universities of applied science, technical universities and standard universities – and each type has a different emphasis on teaching and what it considers architecture to be, with some being more technical or arty than others.

What standard and conceptual understanding of architecture is demanded in each year of architectural education varies wildly across the world. This is in part due to the different points where access to the profession is legislated and controlled – in the United Kingdom this occurs on successful completion of Part 3. However, if you are transferring to a similar course elsewhere, you need to know whether the expectations at any given part of the course are similar to what's expected at the same level in the UK.

Architectural courses in the UK, EU (ECTS) and US are designed on a credit system, which means a crucial thing to consider is the transferrability of any credits you accumulate when you return to your home country. Before embarking on study, ensure that you fully understand what you will gain credits for and how they will contribute to gaining your overall degree. Each unit of study is worth 10 or 20 credits, with a maximum of 60 credits per term.

> **10 UK CREDITS = 5 ECTS CREDITS = 2.5 US CREDITS**
>
> **20 UK CREDITS = 10 ECTS CREDITS = 5 US CREDITS**
>
> **60 UK CREDITS = 30 ECTS CREDITS = 15 US CREDITS**

Similarly, work out what you will learn while abroad and, if you want a UK qualification when you return, how you will bank your credits and work in the UK system. In the UK, each student's graduating portfolio must illustrate compliance with and expertise in the relevant ARB criteria for Parts 1, 2 and 3. As you move out of the UK, the relevant pedagogic requirements change. Students can struggle on returning from a term or semester exchange abroad to accumulate the skills needed in the UK. This is simply because they have not been taught the relevant skillsets abroad and then must rush to achieve them in a shorter time on their return. Talk to your home institution's course director about the learning outcomes your student colleagues will achieve while you are away, and what you will be expected to have mastered on your return to keep pace with them.

Dr Marco Cimillo, Lecturer and Programme Director at Xi'an Jiaotong-Liverpool University describes their international student offer: 'XJTLU offers a unique perspective, from a major heritage centre in the Yangtze Delta, one of the most dynamic megalopolises in the world. All programmes are taught in English by an international team and students can spend one to four semesters abroad, through an exchange scheme or by completing their education at the University of Liverpool.

Home students receive continuous English language support and the international [students] are offered Chinese language courses. The master's results in a British qualification, while the graduates of the bachelor [degree] are awarded both a Chinese and a British degree. Both UK titles are validated by the RIBA.'

The Bartlett at University College London has a student exchange programme with the Southern California Institute of Architecture in Los Angeles. Professor Bob Sheil, Director of the Bartlett School of Architecture at UCL, describes this exchange: 'The Bartlett School of Architecture UCL and Sci-Arc share an annual single-semester exchange programme for up to two master's students from each respective school. Both institutions share common ground for design experimentation and speculative projects with an internationally facing mindset. Both are staffed by a high proportion of part-time tutors who are active as practitioners and researchers, many of whom are regular speakers in schools worldwide. The Bartlett School of Architecture also runs a small number of pop-up workshops in Asia, Europe, and Central and South America, including an annual workshop at the Chinese Academy of Fine Art.'

6.3
Taubman College of Architecture and Planning, University of Michigan, Rui (Shirley) Xu, The Unexpected Journey of Mr. W, Detective Plan, Year 5. **Facilitated by a transition from one media to another, this image articulates an architectural satire that foretells a future run by machine-esque provocateurs. This project addresses real and urgent socio-political, economic and moral concerns linked to the life of the city.**

6.4
University of Portsmouth, Ahmad Khairul
Zaim Bin AB Gafa, Vacci-Nation, Rome.
**A hybrid, multi-use urban intervention,
rejuvenating ancient city fabric and
facilitating new catalytic connections.**

6.5
University of Portsmouth, Peh Ker Nang,
City Within a City, Rome.
**A small piece of a city, any city can
be seen as a microcosm of the larger
whole. This proposal attempts to
condense the frisson of the larger city
to create a new city sector.**

6.6
Taubman College of Architecture and
Planning, University of Michigan,
Invasive Species: Cultivar – Night Shift,
Karl Heckman, Year 5.
A site that is both here and there,
simultaneously. In this politically
active thesis, a rogue Environmental
Protection Agency ark has a double
life – existing as a landform in Canada,
and also populating a Thomas Cole
painting that inconspicuously unpacks
itself into a digitally gilded, and now
nocturnally active, interior of the 'real'
EPA headquarters.

Architect Max Dewdney benefited from an exchange programme with
Cooper Union in New York and later became a Rome Scholar: 'Studying
in Rome and New York allowed me to look at my own culture in new
and critical ways. At the Cooper Union the dialogues with Americans
who had studied European architecture and Europeans in America was
enlightening and opened new perspectives. The curious "newness"
and "oldness" of New York made me question standard histories and
categories of architecture. The gift of Rome is its layered complexity,
which made me appreciate the deep material time of building and design.
Studying abroad taught me to step outside of myself, to search for new
ways to see and create work that can transcend a singular place or time.'

As an example, the University of Portsmouth is particularly encouraging of
incoming and outgoing study-abroad opportunities. It actively encourages
its students to engage with exchange programmes and intercultural
opportunities offered in addition to or as part of its courses. BA and MArch
architecture students, as well as BA interior architecture and design
students, benefit from the school's global network of partners in South
America, Europe, the Middle East and Asia.

Students are offered a range of free language-learning opportunities,
and could start their experiences by attending international field trips
organised at both university and school level. A MArch student from
Portsmouth School of Architecture, who participated in study trips to
Slovenia and China, explained: 'This experience enabled me to take on
more than I thought was possible. Over four weeks I made the most of
the opportunity that had been given to me. I took away new friends, new
language skills, but more importantly new understanding of why things
are done in a specific or different way.'

It's common that a student will wish to travel abroad to study with a
certain teacher/architectural designer because their studio or unit is often
involved in unique work. An example of this global uniqueness of design
emphasis exists in Perry Kulper's studio at Ann Arbor, as it does with
Brian Kelly's Studio at University of Nebraska Lincoln. Kelly has recently
brought his studio to Europe for particularly intense, sustained periods
of months, and describes the importance of studying abroad: 'Immersing
oneself in a different culture and understanding unfamiliar social situations
builds empathy. Students can't rely solely on what they know; they have
to engage. When any student or parent asks why studying abroad is
important, I always tell them it offers exposure to different perspectives,
different cultures, and an understanding that the world is a huge place.'

6.7
University of Nebraska Lincoln, Joshua
Puppe, The Antithesis: Challenging the
Current Execution of University Thesis via
the Exquisite Cappriccio and Grand Tour,
London, Year 6.
This project, inspired by what the
student has experienced in Europe
generally and London particularly,
picks up on and architecturally explores
polemic tropes to question the linear
progression of traditional
architectural projects.

Megan Petersen, one of Kelly's alumni studying abroad, sums it up like this:
'You never realise how much you did not get it until you experience it. Your
mind clicks and you have the chance to find out that before, you actually
had no idea.'

Part 3

Finding a post-Part 2 job, and Part 3

While you are in the final stages of work for your master's, it's important to be aware of work opportunities outside academia. Much like finding a job for your previous 'year out' between undergraduate and postgraduate level, an element of forethought and research is required. Again, the RIBA job board is a suitable starting point, or you might wish to return to the same practice where you did your post-Part 1 work experience. As before, practices can write directly to schools for post-Part 2 students, advertise direct in an architectural journal, on their website or other architectural websites, sometimes even on Instagram. The advice about preparing your portfolio and finding job opportunities mentioned earlier in this book will still be of use. If you already have a job that has been financially sustaining you throughout your studies, talk to your employer about Part 3 and your job roles in relation to it. Talk to the professional studies advisor at your school (if it has one), as they will be able to offer advice and will know about good practice for Part 3 support and mentoring.

Founding Director of Heneghan Peng, Roisin Heneghan, explains what they look for in a Part 2 graduate at interview: 'A developed sense of beauty in everything they do, from how they present their CV to their portfolio. Ability to express their architectural project visually, in drawing and models, coupled with an enquiring approach to their work and what they have been asked to do.'

RIBA Jobs (jobs.architecture.com) is a great way to start your search online. It features relevant positions for Part 1, Part 2 and Part 3 students with RIBA architects and chartered practices. Representing roles from a full range of offices across the UK and internationally – small and large, in rural and urban areas – it enables you to think about the type of practice where you might want to gain vital experience in the first few years of your career.

You need a practice that will encourage, mentor and support you in getting the experience and information you will need to complete further studies. As such, it's recommended to research the criteria for Part 3.

The size of an office is important, as it often determines the sort of experience you will get. A smaller office might have smaller, simpler jobs; a medium to large office might offer experience of a different organisational structure and larger, more complex work. The bigger the projects you work on, the more some of your experience might be observational. It's important to understand how an office works, and whether the office understands the obligations you and it have towards one another at Part 3 level. Choose your practice wisely.

7.1
Royal College of Art, Live Project at Manifesta12, Year 4.
Often students are encouraged to make their architecture at 1:1 scale and bring it to its site, to engage the site and its users. This can also be combined with theatrical performance.

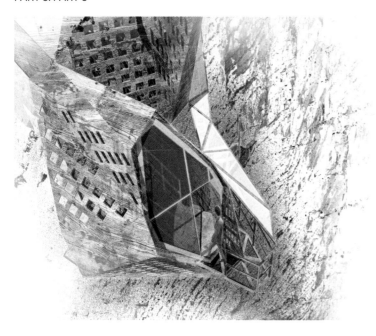

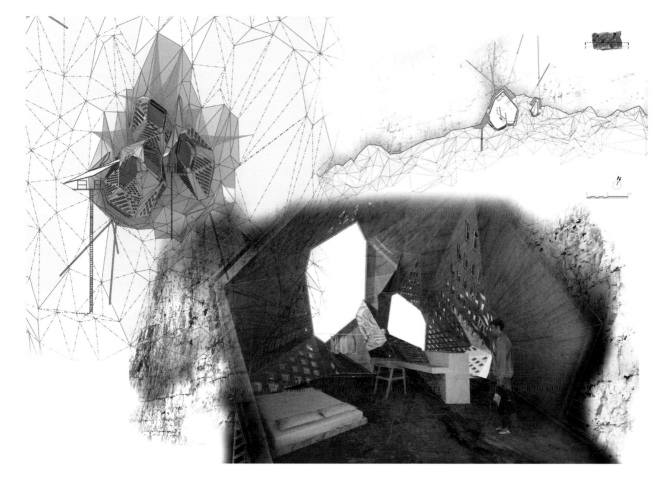

Part 3

<u>WHY PART 3?</u>
Professor Stephen Brookhouse, author of *Part 3 Handbook*

Part 3 is the final part of your architectural education. It uses your experience as a young designer working in architectural practice on real projects to explore the business of delivering design. Making buildings is a team effort – bringing together architects and other design and construction professionals. Part 3 aims to give you an understanding of how you as an architect can contribute to taking sustainable design 'beyond the studio' and making a difference to the future built environment.

What distinguishes an architect who has undertaken Part 3 from an architectural designer who only has Part 2?

Part 3 is the gateway to the profession of architecture – and because the title 'architect' is protected in the UK, you cannot call yourself an architect without having passed Part 3. More importantly, it is recognised globally by governments, clients, the professional team and the public. Architecture is more than creating designs – it's about making them happen. Because your qualification as an architect is recognised internationally, everyone understands and respects the high level of your education, your achievements and ability to think creatively as a professional, and your ability to contribute effectively to delivering sustainable design. As an architect you will also enjoy the support of fellow architects – and the professional institutes – in the development of your career and in meeting the many challenges ahead.

Professional practice at Part 3 is the final stage towards registering as an architect. Paul Crosby, the Architectural Association's Part 3 Course Head, succinctly describes its scope and timing: 'Having completed five years' undergraduate and postgraduate academic studies, the student [may then] gain practical experience in an architect's office. Ideally, after a few months in practice, the student attends a Part 3 course part-time. Having assimilated knowledge with practical experience, the student sits the examination, which includes scenario-based problems and a case study of a project in the office. Key subjects include business management, professionalism and ethics, legal and regulatory frameworks, and communication skills – all of which are essential to the role of an architect.'

7.2, 7.3
London South Bank University,
Wing Hang Tang, experimental living area,
Year 5.
Students are encouraged to explore new ways of living and dwelling. This could be using new technologies or materials, or imagining different family or social hierarchies.

CHOOSING A PART 3 COURSE

Part 3 is very different from Parts 1 and 2. It is intended to augment and assess your professional skills: all the other skills that are needed for an architect to build a building above and beyond design.

Every qualified architect has been through a Part 3 course and successfully graduated from it. Part 3 changes, as do all courses, so initially talk to architects or students who have recently been on or are currently on a Part 3 course. Ask them questions about how satisfied they were with their course. What did they learn from it? Was it rewarding and confidence boosting? How was it delivered? How much time did they spend on it? What were the methods of assessment? How much did it cost? How engaged were the staff? Did your office pay their fees?

Part 3 is delivered academically in different ways, where some schools deliver it for an evening a week, while others deliver it as concentrated short courses. Part 3 courses are provided by most schools of architecture; some, such as the courses from the Liverpool, Manchester and Northumbria schools, are delivered by the RIBA from the RIBA North office, while APEAS delivers Part 3 for the Scottish schools of architecture.

PART 3 CURRICULUM

The Part 3 curriculum is based around the following five areas:

1. **Professionalism:** Acting ethically, with integrity, competence and judgement.
2. **Clients, users and delivery of services:** Delivering professional services and working effectively with clients and other stakeholders.
3. **Legal framework and processes:** Working effectively within the legal and regulatory context.
4. **Practice and management:** Managing processes to meet business requirements.
5. **Building procurement:** Procuring and managing services to deliver construction projects.

Part 3 is logically organised and arranged into a small series of activities and academic outputs that allow you to illustrate and reflect on your architectural journey to date and demonstrate your problem-solving abilities in relation to professional standards and protocols. These are:

*   An illustrated CV
*   Career appraisal
*   Evidence of 24 months' approved and documented professional experience (PEDR)
*   Written examinations and/or coursework assignments
*   Professional case study (a few courses do not require a case study)
*   Oral examination with professional examiners

Be clear on how your Part 3 course delivers these requirements in terms of the demands and timescale relative to your experience, as well as the support you will need both from your office and the staff of the course itself. It's also important to choose a course that is convenient for you and can fit in with your home and work life. For example, you might prefer a course that has a continuous assessment regime and no exams, or vice versa.

Fees vary and are dependent on the length and mode of delivery, so it is important to understand the fee structure of your chosen Part 3 provider.

In contrast to your professional studies conducted at Part 2, Part 3 will introduce you to real-world case studies and examples of all manner of subjects, including legal and contractual frameworks, land and property law, how to write contractual letters to clients, fellow consultants and contractors, and architectural management skills. In other words, it should cover all professional skills, management protocols and legal obligations for every stage of architectural work from appointment to post-occupancy analysis.

Recently qualified architect Natalie Gall recounts the structure of her Part 3: 'I undertook my Part 3 at Kingston University and I have to say this may have been my favourite part of all three parts. This surprised even me, as typically I was better known for hand drawing through Part 1 and Part 2; however it was then that I realised that I found law really interesting. I actually enjoyed the black and white nature of a contract. My favourite task was going through scenarios and deciding what the architect's actions should be. Halfway through my Part 3 I thought to myself "how on earth did I do my job without knowing all of this?!"'

You require 24 months of practical training before taking the Part 3 examination. The length of time may vary but the aim is to have an adequate knowledge and understanding – rather than direct experience – of the subject areas covered by the Part 3 professional criteria. Offices are generally very supportive, as all architects have been through the process. Peter Morris observes: 'We encourage our Part 2 graduates not to rush into their Part 3. We cover the cost of Part 3 course fees and offer 10 days' study leave per year of study. An associate director acts as Part 3 coordinator and students are encouraged to form study groups. More experienced architects will act as mentors throughout the student's Part 3 programme'.

Although you do not need experience across a whole project, Heneghan Peng take another approach: 'We want people to go through all aspects of a project from concept to construction. For people doing Part 3, we try to organise the team so that they can take one aspect and lead that on site (under the project architect), for example concrete, facade or services.'

Understanding the different procurement and contractual routes under which the office is delivering architecture is important, as it helps to learn where your evolving experience might be lacking from job to job. For example, a design and build contract is very different from more traditional contracts, and the architect's role changes as a result. Equally, you will learn more about other valuable subjects, from how clients appoint architects to dealing with other professionals, local planning offices, health and safety, and the wellbeing of the public who use buildings.

Each Part 3 course has a different way of meeting the Part 3 professional criteria. A key aspect of Part 3 is for the student to make it not just a reflective, retrospective analysis of where they've been and what they've learned, but also to project forward and imagine where they want their career to go how to develop their strengths, preoccupations and ambitions. *Part 3 Handbook* by Stephen Brookhouse is the recognised authority text on RIBA Part 3.

When you complete your Part 3, you can apply join the Architects' Register and become a Chartered Member of the RIBA. You deserve full congratulations – studying architecture has probably taken a decade or more, and you have proved you are a professional, with all that entails.

Having spent seven years on a path leading to this moment, and always knowing the exact next step, it can be strange to have nothing in front of you. It can be worthwhile formulating plans, or aims, for the next three to five years to focus your energy on working hard and building a portfolio.

But never stop 'designing' your career. As Robin Cross, international development architect, observes: 'It took me about 20 years to make my career what I always wanted it to be.'

Continuing professional development

The pursuit of architecture as a profession is a life-long learning experience. To continue to have a meaningful engagement with the profession and cope with all the changes that will come in your professional career, it is important to continuously update your skills and knowledge. The RIBA and many other stakeholders provide a variety of continuing professional development (CPD) courses.

Joni Tyler, Head of CPD at the RIBA, comments: 'Doing (and recording) continuing professional development (CPD) is obligatory for RIBA Chartered Members. In fact, CPD is now a regular part of working life for people in any sector. But more than an obligation, the right CPD is also beneficial to your career and your business. Doing CPD helps you to stay competent, professional, capable and resilient as an architect. CPD enables you to achieve better outcomes and better businesses. CPD also helps you to contend with disruption and to face current and future challenges as well as learn new skills and specialisms.'

Completing Part 3

So, you are now an architect ...

You are now well equipped to make a lasting contribution not only to the architectural profession, but also to society as a whole. As your career develops you must remember to design your pathway through the profession, maximising your strengths and skills. These skills may not necessarily be in design or architectural visualisation – they could equally well be in job running, contract management, securing work, or a mixture of all these and other activities. Good luck – there is always a bit of luck involved – and seize every opportunity with optimism, worldliness and a kind heart.

Five ways to get ahead

1. Develop your portfolio for interview, This should mix academic work with the most interesting project work from your previous year out.
2. Talk to your network about who is good to work for and supportive of Part 3 students.
3. Once in a job, make sure you get the right experience and fill in your PEDR regularly.
4. Reflect on what you have learned in your architecture career to date, and know where your blind spots are. Pick a Part 3 course that will let you see into these blind spots.
5. Develop a career plan, for the next three to five years.

APPENDIX 1

SELECTED USEFUL REFERENCES

BOOKS ON BUILDINGS AND URBAN DESIGN

Kenneth Frampton, *Modern Architecture: A Critical History,* Thames and Hudson, 2007

Jonathan Glancey, *Architecture: A Visual History,* DK, 2017

Thom Mayne and Eui-Sung Yi, *100 Buildings,* Rizzoli, 2017

Will Pryce, *World Architecture: The Masterworks,* Thames and Hudson, 2011

BOOKS ON HISTORY, THEORY AND FUTURES

Mark Garcia, *The Diagrams of Architecture,* Wiley, 2010 – an excellent springboard to this area of study

Charles Jencks and Karl Kropf, *Theories and Manifestos of Contemporary Architecture,* Wiley-Academy, 1997

Neil Spiller, *Visionary Architecture – Blueprints of the Modern Imagination,* Thames and Hudson, 2006 – for a history of visionary architecture of the twentieth century

BOOKS ON SKETCHING, DRAWING AND DIGITAL DRAWING

Francis D. Ching, *Architectural Graphics,* Wiley, 2015

Peter Cook, *Drawing: The Motive Force of Architecture,* Wiley, 2013

Mathew Frederick, *101 Things I Learned at Architecture School,* MIT Press, 2007

Mathew Frederick, *101 Things I Learned in Urban Design School*, MIT Press, 2018

Will Jones, *Architects' Sketchbooks,* Thames and Hudson, 2011

Will Jones, *Making Marks: Architects' Sketchbooks – The Creative Process,* Thames and Hudson, 2019

Frank Melendez, *Drawing from the Model: Fundamentals of Digital Drawing, 3D Modeling, and Visual Programming in Architectural Design,* Wiley, 2019

Susan C. Piedmont-Palladino, *How Drawings Work: A User Friendly Theory,* Routledge, 2019

Douglas R. Seidler, *Digital Drawing for Designers: A Visual Guide to AutoCAD® 2017,* Bloomsbury, 2016

Neil Spiller, *Drawing Architecture (Architectural Design),* Wiley, 2013

Helen Thomas, *Drawing Architecture,* Phaidon, 2018

CONSTRUCTION AND STRUCTURE

Francis. D. Ching, *Building Construction Illustrated, 5th Edition,* Wiley, 2014

Francis. D. Ching, *Building Structures Illustrated: Patterns, Systems, and Design, 2nd Edition,* Wiley, 2014

Stephen Emmitt, *Barry's Introduction to the Construction of Buildings,* Wiley, 2018

ESSAY WRITING

How to write different types of essay: www.teachervision.com/writing/sample-essay-outlines

A. and J. Lange, *Writing about Architecture: Mastering the Language of Buildings and Cities,* Princeton Architectural Press, 2012

George Orwell, *Politics and the English Language,* 1946: www.orwell.ru/library/essays/politics/english/e_polit

L. Truss, *Eats, Shoots and Leaves: The Zero Tolerance Approach to Punctuation,* HarperCollins, 2017

C. Wiseman, *Writing Architecture: A Practical Guide to Clear Communication about the Built Environment,* Trinity University Press, 2017

FINANCIAL MATTERS

RIBA Support Fund: www.architecture.com/education-cpd-and-careers/studying-architecture/advice-on-funding-your-architectural-studies/funding-opportunities-for-students-of-architecture/riba-student-support-fund

Make sure you have approached your university hardship fund and all other funds that the university might have access to. **Receiving maintenance grants and loans does not disqualify you from applying for university hardship support. University hardship funds also look only at your personal financial situation and not that of your parents.** Please approach your university for support if you have not done so already. Funds should not discriminate based on nationality unless this will impact on immigration status. Contact your alumni fund, too, as these will often have support schemes in place.

www.gov.uk/extra-money-pay-university/university-and-college-hardship-funds
www.gov.uk/browse/education/student-finance

Look to exhaust all other methods of funding. **Charities and government grants** are available and often small charities will support you if you fall within their remit, even without a scheme announced. **Do approach any charities in your locality** such as the local Rotary Clubs of other similar organisations.

Websites with alternative lists of support:

www.thestudentroom.co.uk/wiki/Funding_Postgraduate_Study – guide to funding
grants-search.turn2us.org.uk – list of charities
www.scholarship-search.org.uk – list of scholarship schemes across the UK
www.postgraduate-funding.com – list of alternative funding, requires registration

If you have one year of work experience working in architecture practice in the UK, please contact the **Architects Benevolent Society,** as they might be able to help you. Support is available to everyone who experiences poverty, and is tailored to individual needs: www.absnet.org.uk/

If you are **struggling to fund a field trip,** please negotiate with your department. There should be some support, or the university course should be able to provide you with a low-cost alternative to the field trip. No field trip should be mandatory in the UK; the RIBA does not stipulate such requirements. Whereas any travel is always beneficial, this should not push you into hardship.

Part-time work can be a way of supplementing your income, and you can work alongside your studies within reason. The official advice is no more than 20 hours per week. There are many **local job shops,** university jobs and other work. Useful websites to explore are www.peopleperhour.com and www.fiverr.com for tasks which can be done remotely and part-time. Universities often hire students as ambassadors or for other work, so **seek support internally.**

Apply for other **RIBA scholarships** on a merit basis: www.architecture.com/education-cpd-and-careers/studying-architecture/advice-on-funding-your-architectural-studies/funding-opportunities-for-students-of-architecture

FINDING A JOB

RIBA Jobs:
RIBA Jobs is one of the most popular job boards for architecture and design-related roles. It is perfect for job-seeking students, as it advertises positions at all levels, including Part 1, Part 2 and Part 3. It allows you to seek out roles from premier RIBA practices by proactively signing up to job alerts. RIBA Jobs provides opportunities with a full range of offices from well-known, global practices to boutique local studios. It features jobs in rural areas and regional cities as well as in London and overseas: jobs.architecture.com

FIRST YEAR

Free RIBA Student Membership:
www.architecture.com/join-riba/free-student-membership

Information regarding the RIBA student mentoring scheme:
www.architecture.com/education-cpd-and-careers/studying-architecture/student-mentoring

Learning how to use Photoshop:
hiphopmakers.com/free-adobe-photoshop-tutorials-for-beginners

FUNDING

General advice on funding your architectural education:
www.architecture.com/education-cpd-and-careers/studying-architecture/advice-on-funding-your-architectural-studies

Do you want to complete Part 1 and 2 while working in an office?
www.architecture.com/education-cpd-and-careers/studying-architecture/riba-studio

Apprenticeships in architecture:
www.architecture.com/campaign/apprenticeships
www.ribaj.com/intelligence/architecture-apprenticeships-course-round-up-fosters-eleanor-young

Student Loans Company:
www.slc.co.uk

GETTING TO SCHOOL

Find out what an architect does on a day-to-day basis:
www.lifeofanarchitect.com/what-does-an-architect-do/
www.his.com/~pshapiro/architects.html

A succinct introduction to the various pathways to becoming an architect:
www.architecture.com/education-cpd-and-careers/how-to-become-an-architect

Think Architecture is a virtual RIBA magazine with useful articles, for people thinking of becoming architects:
www.architecture.com/-/media/files/Education/Think-Architecture-PDF.pdf

Introductory RIBA workshops for those interested in architecture:
www.architecture.com/education-cpd-and-careers/learning

Research appropriate architecture schools through open days and taster days, school websites and social media:
unistats.ac.uk

Lists of RIBA-validated schools in the UK and overseas, and the procedures and criteria they have to meet:
www.architecture.com/education-cpd-and-careers/riba-validation

UCAS main website, with advice on university applications and student loans:
www.ucas.com

UCAS tariff points:
www.ucas.com/undergraduate/what-and-where-study/entry-requirements/ucas-tariff-points

MENTAL WELLBEING

RIBA mental health advice:
www.architecture.com/knowledge-and-resources/knowledge-landing-page/architecture-students-mental-health
Architects Benevolent Society's student mental health support:
absnet.org.uk/need-help/how-we-help/mental-health-support/student-mental-health-support#overlay-context=students

MIND – The Mental Health Charity:
www.mind.org.uk
www.mind.org.uk/information-support/tips-for-everyday-living/student-life/#.XLdcb6R7IPY

Ben Channon, *Happy by Design: A Guide to Architecture and Mental Wellbeing,* RIBA Publishing, 2018

Mental health support is available for students on all degrees: absnet.org.uk/need-help/how-we-help/mental-health-support. Please contact your local NHS and your university's services as well if you are experiencing mental health issues; however, if they are slow to respond, the ABS can provide support. Other mental health support is provided by charities such as Student Minds: www.studentminds.org.uk

SUPPORTING DIVERSITY

Accessing Architecture: Starting Out is a suite of guidance documents to support people with disabilities entering or progressing in careers in architecture. 'Starting Out' is written for students, career advisors and guardians: www.architecture.com/-/media/gathercontent/accessing-architecture/additional-documents/accessingarchitecture1startingoutpdf.pdf

Architecture for All: Celebrating Architecture with The Architecture Foundation – is a short documentary exploring diversity in architecture and the decline of creative education in the UK: www.architecturefoundation.org.uk/film/architecture-for-all

Architecture LGBT+ provides a safe, inclusive and prejudice-free environment for LGBT+ architects and those working and studying within the profession. This is done through networking events, learning, mentoring and role models: www.architecturelgbt.com

Black Females in Architecture (BFA) is a network to make black women more visible in the built environment sector. Founded in 2018, BFA now has over 150 members sharing advice on WhatsApp and at organised workshops: @BlackFemArch

The Built by Us FLUID Diversity Mentoring Programme addresses retention and development of practitioners from diverse backgrounds for management and leadership roles in the sector. It links volunteer mentors and mentees from across the construction industry to enable the support and development of the mentee. Construction professionals at a variety of career stages are encouraged to take part. The programme has been developed to address the under-representation within management and leadership structures in the built environment sector. It mainly focuses on women, BAME groups, people with disabilities, LGBT people and those from low socio-economic backgrounds: www.builtbyus.org.uk/fluid

Building Equality is an alliance of construction organisations and professionals working together to drive LGBT+ inclusion in the construction sector. Over the past five years they have rapidly grown and expanded their reach from London into regional hubs in Leeds and Manchester: www.rics.org/uk/news-insight/latest-news/news-opinion/building-equality

Build Up runs practical construction projects for people aged 6–20 to design and build structures in their local communities. Since 2014, it has supported over 800 disadvantaged young people. The charity has been awarded grant funding through the Mayor's Crowdfund London programme which will go towards constructing a new public space in Hackney: www.buildup.org.uk

The DisOrdinary Architecture Project has been working with architectural and built environment practitioners for over a decade. It aims to open practices to more creative and critical engagement with disability, ability, access and inclusion through collaboration: disordinaryarchitecture.com/wp

freeholdLGBT is a networking forum for LGBT+ built environment professionals. Members include surveyors, asset managers, architects, developers, investors and property lawyers: united-kingdom.taylorwessing.com/en/services/services/level3/freehold

InterEngineering is an organisation that promotes LGBT diversity and inclusion within engineering. It has regional groups across the UK: interengineeringlgbt.com

MATT+FIONA is a collaborative venture which ensures young people have a say in the spaces and buildings that they use every day. Each project has a clear pathway: briefing, design and build, with the children and young people at the centre of every stage. Examples of projects include enabling Year 6 at Lansbury Lawrence Primary School to design, develop and build their own community art room in Poplar. Children with autism at Phoenix School were also supported to create their own playground shelter on their new school site in Bow: mattandfiona.org

Missing in Architecture is a collection of architects and educators who want to promote creativity and action within the profession, interested in filling in the gaps in architecture by producing socially and politically provocative pieces, engaging with the community and council and everyone in between: www.missinginarchitecture.net

Open City Learning Programmes – Accelerate is a pioneering education and mentoring programme created in 2012 by Open City in partnership with the Bartlett School of Architecture. It's aimed at Year 12 students to increase diversity in the architecture profession. Seventy per cent of Accelerate participants have secured conditional offers to study architecture and related subjects at university. These include University College London (UCL), the University of Cambridge and the University of Manchester: open-city.org.uk/learning

Paradigm Network exists to support, encourage and help talented architects from BAME backgrounds in education and as they progress in their careers: www.paradigmnetwork.co.uk

Part W is a women's action group that instigates new forms of discussion and debate around the issue of inequality in the built environment: @PartWCollective

Planning Out is a network for LGBT+ planners. It supports the 'second wave' of LGBT+ rights where gay people at work have the same level of acceptance and dignity as everyone else: @PlanningOut

Society of Black Architects (SOBA) is a group advocating for black architects' rights, opportunities and visibility.

Stephen Lawrence Charitable Trust aims to be a fitting legacy to Stephen's memory and to make a real impact by supporting young people to transform their lives by overcoming disadvantage and discrimination and moving into ambitious careers as professionals.

Stephen Lawrence Day Educational Materials – library of resources to help plan community or school activities for the annual Stephen Lawrence Day on or around 22 April. Materials include posters, social action toolkit, assembly scripts and reading lists. www.stephenlawrence.org.uk/stephen-lawrence-day/resources

Stephen Lawrence Trust Building Futures – the programme includes outreach and visits to local schools to create awareness of architecture, design and engineering careers and the support the trust can offer students; work experience placements at the studio where the students are given a design brief for a project based in their local area; site visits and research activities, drawing, model making, 3D visualisation and Revit workshops; CV/portfolio training; and mock interviews to prepare for university applications. All students who take part can apply for a bursary to that helps to cover fees and living expenses for university: www.stephenlawrence.org.uk/what-we-do/built-environment

Urbanistas is collaborative women-led network amplifying women's voices and ideas to make cities better for everyone: www.urbanistas.org.uk

SELECTED USEFUL REFERENCES

YEARS OUT, PROFESSIONAL EXPERIENCE
AND DEVELOPMENT

Professional Education and Development Record (PEDR):
www.architecture.com/pedr

RIBA Plan of Work (Appendix 2):
www.architecture.com/knowledge-and-resources/resources-landing-page/riba-plan-of-work

Stephen Brookhouse, *Part 3 Handbook,* RIBA Publishing, 2014

Stephen Brookhouse, *Professional Studies in Architecture: A Primer,*
RIBA Publishing, 2013

The RIBA has its own Part 3 course:
www.architecture.com/education-cpd-and-careers/studying-architecture/riba-part-3

Adrian Dobson, *21 Things You Won't Learn in Architecture School,*
RIBA Publishing, 2014

RIBA Continuing Professional Development (CPD):
www.architecture.com/education-cpd-and-careers/cpd

Architects Registration Board:
www.arb.org.uk

APPENDIX 2

RIBA
Plan of Work
2020

The RIBA Plan of Work organises the process of briefing, designing, delivering, maintaining, operating and using a building into eight stages. It is a framework for all disciplines on construction projects and should be used solely as guidance for the preparation of detailed professional services and building contracts.

0
Strategic Definition

1
Preparation and Briefing

2
Concept Design

◄------------------ Projects span from Stage 1 to Stage 6, the

Stage Boundaries:

Stages 0–4 will generally be undertaken one after the other.

Stages 4 and 5 will overlap in the Project Programme for most projects.

Stage 5 commences when the contractor takes possession of the site and finishes at **Practical Completion.**

Stage 6 starts with the handover of the building to the client immediately after **Practical Completion** and finishes at the end of the **Defects Liability Period.**

Stage 7 starts concurrently with Stage 6 and lasts for the life of the building.

Procurement:

The RIBA Plan of Work is procurement neutral – See Overview Guidance for a detailed description of how each stage might be adjusted to accommodate the requirements of the **Procurement Strategy.**

 ER Employers Requirements

 CP Contractors Proposals

	0 Strategic Definition	**1 Preparation and Briefing**	**2 Concept Design**
Stage Outcome at the end of the stage	The best means of achieving the **Client Requirements** confirmed ⬝ If the outcome determines that a building is the best means of achieving the **Client Requirements**, the client proceeds to stage 1	**Project Brief** approved by the client and confirmed that it can be accommodated on the site	**Architectural Concept** approved by the client and aligned to the **Project Brief** ⬝ The brief remains "live" during Stage 2 and is derogated in response to the **Architectural Concept**
Core Tasks during the stage	Prepare **Client Requirements** ⬝ Develop **Business Case** for feasible options including review of **Project Risks** and **Project Budget** ⬝ Ratify option that best delivers **Client Requirements** ⬝ Review **Feedback** from previous projects ⬝ Undertake **Site Appraisals**	Prepare **Project Brief** including **Project Outcomes** and **Sustainability Outcomes, Quality Aspirations** and **Spatial Requirements** ⬝ Undertake **Feasibility Studies** ⬝ Agree **Project Budget** ⬝ Source **Site Information** including **Site Surveys** ⬝ Prepare **Project Programme** ⬝ Prepare **Project Execution Plan**	Prepare **Architectural Concept** incorporating **Strategic Engineering** requirements and aligned to **Cost Plan, Project Strategies** and **Outline Specification** ⬝ Agree **Project Brief** derogations ⬝ Undertake **Design Reviews** with client and **Project Stakeholders** ⬝ Prepare stage **Design Programme**
	Project Strategies might include: – Conservation (if applicable) – Cost – Fire Safety – Health and Safety – Inclusive Design – Planning – Plan for Use – Procurement – Sustainability See *RIBA Plan of Work 2020* Overview for detailed guidance on **Project Strategies**	No design team required for Stages 0 and 1. Client advisers may be appointed to the client team to provide strategic advice and design thinking before Stage 2 commences.	
Core Statutory Processes during the stage: Planning Building Regulations Health and Safety (CDM)	Strategic appraisal of **Planning** considerations	Source pre-application **Planning Advice** ⬝ Initiate collation of health and safety **Pre-construction Information**	Obtain pre-application **Planning Advice** ⬝ Agree route to **Building Regulations** compliance ⬝ Option: submit outline **Planning Application**
Procurement Route Traditional Design & Build 1 Stage Design & Build 2 Stage Management Contract Construction Management Contractor-led	Appoint client team	Appoint design team	ER ⬝ Appoint contractor ⬝ ER
Information Exchanged at the end of the stage	Client Requirements Business Case	Project Brief Feasibility Studies Site Information Project Budget Project Programme Procurement Strategy Responsibility Matrix Information Requirements	Project Brief derogations Signed off **Stage Report** **Project Strategies** Outline Specification Cost Plan

RIBA
Architecture.com

Core RIBA Plan of Work terms are defined in the *RIBA Plan of Work 2020 Overview* glossary and set in **Bold Type.**

3 Spatial Coordination	**4** Technical Design	**5** Manufacturing and Construction	**6** Handover	**7** Use

outcome of Stage 0 may be the decision to initiate a project and Stage 7 covers the ongoing use of the building. ➡

Architectural and engineering information **Spatially Coordinated**	All design information required to manufacture and construct the project completed	Manufacturing, construction and commissioning completed	Building handed over, **Aftercare** initiated and **Building Contract** concluded	Efficient use, operation and maintenance of building
	Stage 4 will overlap with Stage 5 on most projects	There is no design work in Stage 5 other than responding to **Site Queries**		Stage 7 starts concurrently with Stage 6 and lasts for the life of the building

Undertake **Design Studies, Engineering Analysis** and **Cost Exercises** to test **Architectural Concept** resulting in **Spatially Coordinated Design** aligned to updated **Cost Plan, Project Strategies** and **Outline Specification** Initiate **Change Control Procedures** Prepare stage **Design Programme**	Develop architectural and engineering technical design Prepare and coordinate design team **Building Systems** information Prepare and integrate specialist subcontractor **Building Systems** information Prepare stage **Design Programme**	Finalise **Site Logistics** Manufacture **Building Systems** and construct building Monitor progress against **Construction Programme** Inspect **Construction Quality** Resolve **Site Queries** as required Commission building Prepare **Building Manual**	Hand over building in line with **Plan for Use Strategy** Undertake **Project Feedback** Undertake seasonal commissioning Rectify defects Complete initial **Aftercare** tasks including light touch **Post Occupancy Evaluation**	Implement **Facility** and **Asset Management** Undertake **Post Occupancy Evaluation** of building performance in use Verify **Project Outcomes** including **Sustainability Outcomes**
	Specialist subcontractor designs are prepared and reviewed during Stage 4	Building handover tasks bridge Stages 5 and 6 as set out in the **Plan for Use Strategy**		Adaptation of a building (at the end of its useful life) triggers a new Stage 0

Review design against **Building Regulations** Prepare and submit **Planning Application**	Submit **Building Regulations Application** Discharge pre-commencement **Planning Conditions** Prepare **Construction Phase Plan** Submit F10 to HSE if applicable	Carry out **Construction Phase Plan** Comply with **Planning Conditions** related to construction	Comply with **Planning Conditions** as required	Comply with **Planning Conditions** as required
See *Planning Note* for guidance on submitting a **Planning Application** earlier than at end of Stage 3				

	Tender / ER CP / Pre-contract services agreement — CP / Preferred bidder — CP : Appoint contractor			Appoint **Facilities Management** and **Asset Management** team, and strategic advisers as needed

Signed off **Stage Report** **Project Strategies** Updated **Outline Specification** Updated **Cost Plan** **Planning Application**	**Manufacturing Information** **Construction Information** **Final Specifications** Residual **Project Strategies** **Building Regulations Application**	**Building Manual** including **Health and Safety File** and **Fire Safety Information** **Practical Completion** certificate including **Defects List** **Asset Information**	**Project Feedback** **Final Certificate** Light touch **Post Occupancy Evaluation** feedback	**Post Occupancy Evaluation** feedback Updated **Building Manual** including **Health and Safety File** and **Fire Safety Information** as necessary
		If **Verified Construction Information** is required, verification tasks must be defined		

Further guidance and detailed stage descriptions are included in the *RIBA Plan of Work 2020 Overview*.

© RIBA 2020

IMAGE CREDITS & INDEX

IMAGE CREDITS

INTRODUCTION

0.1 Ruth McNickle/Edinburgh School of
  Architecture and Landscape Architecture

CHAPTER 1

1.1 Photo Carol Robertson/University of Dundee; 1.2 Edmund Morgan/
University of Brighton; 1.3 Law Yik Yung/University of Strathclyde;
1.4 Sarah Brooke/University of Greenwich; 1.5 Photo Itea Mourla
/ University of Strathclyde; 1.6 Photo Sean O'Tiarnaigh/University
of Dundee; 1.7 Andreas Stadlmayr/University of East London; 1.8
Oliver Flew/University of Coventry; 1.9 Will Haynes/Birmingham City
University; 1.10 Photo Stonehouse Photographic/Bartlett, University
College London; 1.11 Simona Moneva/University of Greenwich; 1.12
Photo Stonehouse Photographic Bartlett Workshop/Bartlett, University
College London; 1.13 Paride Saraceni/University of Greenwich; 1.14
Alex Abadjieva/Edinburgh School of Architecture and Landscape
Architecture; 11.5 Royal College of Art; 1.16 University of East London

CHAPTER 2

2.1 James Kenn/University of Greenwich; 2.2-2.3 Laura Krumina/University
of Strathclyde; 2.4 Ellie Spencer/London South Bank University; 2.5
Diana Grigorie/Birmingham City University; 2.6 George Wade/University
of Coventry; 2.7 Rebecca Sun/Edinburgh School of Architecture and
Landscape Architecture; 2.8 Eugene Yu Jin Soh/University of East
London; 2.9 Kalin Petrov/University of East London; 2.10 Immanuel
Lavery/University of Dundee; 2.11-2.12 Photo Stonehouse Photographic/
Bartlett, University College London; 2.13-2.15 Rebecca Sun/Edinburgh
School of Architecture and Landscape Architecture; 2.16-2.20 Maria
Wolonciej/Edinburgh School of Architecture and Landscape Architecture;
2.21 Photo Graham Whitby Boot/Bartlett, University College London;
2.22 Photo Mark Runnacles/University of Strathclyde; 2.23 Photo Lilly
Kudic/London South Bank University; 2.24 Photo Itea Mourla/University
of Strathclyde; 2.25 Photo David Christian/Royal College of Art

CHAPTER 3

3.1 Annabelle Tan Kai Lin/Bartlett, University College London; 3.2
Eugene Kandinsky/University of Brighton; 3.3-3.4 Ahmed Hamid/
Birmingham City University; 3.5 Hadi Aaseem Pirmohamed/University
of Coventry; 3.6-3.7 Muneeb Kahn/London South Bank University;
3.8-3.9 Mary Leak/University of Strathclyde; 3.10 Grey Grierson/
Bartlett, University College London; 3.11 Agata Malinowska/University
of Brighton; 3.12 Eva Chung/University of Coventry; 3.13-3.16 Photo
Benz Kotzen/University of Dundee; 3.17 Waad Darzi/London South
Bank University; 3.18 Alexander Wilford/University of Greenwich

CHAPTER 4

4.1 Owen Nagy/University of Greenwich; 4.2 Caillin Broatch/
University of Strathclyde; 4.3 Photo Fred Howarth; 4.4-4.5 Photo
Cullinan Studio; 4.6-4.7 Photo Fred Howarth; 4.8 Photo Cullinan
Studio; 4.9-4.10 Paul Leonard/RIBA Studio Diploma

CHAPTER 5

5.1 Jessica Barton/Edinburgh School of Architecture and Landscape
Architecture; 5.2 Tasnim Eshraqi Najafabadi/Bartlett, University College
London; 5.3 David Pow/University of Greenwich; 5.4 William Bryan/
University of Greenwich; 5.5 Imran Sammee/University of Brighton; 5.6
Rebecca Bubb/University of Coventry; 5.7 Edward Crump/University of
Brighton; 5.8 Christopher McCallum, Rishabh Shah and Callum Rowland/
Edinburgh School of Architecture and Landscape Architecture; 5.9 Eugenio
Cappuccio/Mackintosh School of Architecture; 5.10 Boon Wei Phum/
University of East London; 5.11 William Bryan/University of Strathclyde;
5.12 Law Yik Yung/University of Greenwich; 5.13 Marilia Lezou/University
of Greenwich; 5.14 Christopher Sejer Fischlein/Royal College of Art; 5.15
Sonia Magdziarz/Bartlett, University College London; 5.16 James Lawton/
University of Greenwich; 5.17 Eyal Geovannetti/Architectural Association;
5.18 Yakim Milev/London South Bank University; 5.19 Evangelia
Giannoulaki and Marina Konstantopoulou/University of Strathclyde; 5.20
James Dalley/Mackintosh School of Architecture; 5.21-5.22 Livia Wang/
Royal College of Art; 5.23 Selvei Al-Assadi/London South Bank University;
5.24 Liam Bedwell/University of Greenwich; 5.25-5.26 Livia Wang/Royal
College of Art; 5.27 Ryan Cook/Architectural Association; 5.28 Michael On/
University of East London; 5.29 Michael Gibbs/University of Greenwich

CHAPTER 6

6.1-6.2 Xi'an Jiaotong-Liverpool University; 6.3 Rui (Shirley) Xu/
Taubman College of Architecture and Planning, University of Michigan;
6.4 Ahmad Khairul Zaim Bin AB Gafa/University of Portsmouth;
6.5 Peh Ker Nang/University of Portsmouth; 6.6 Karl Heckman/
Taubman College of Architecture and Planning, University of
Michigan; 6.7 Joshua Puppe/University of Nebraska-Lincoln

CHAPTER 7

7.1 Royal College of Art; 7.2-7.3 Wing Hang Tang/
  London South Bank University

Page numbers in **bold** indicate tables.

A Levels 6, 26
academic currency 98
accommodation, schedules of 35, 64, 87
accommodation, student 18, 64
Accreditation of Prior Experiential Learning
    (APEL) 16
applications
    job 93–98, 149
    postgraduate study 108–109
    see also undergraduate application process
apprenticeships **13, 14,** 15, 103, 106
Architects' Register 154
Architects Registration Board (ARB) criteria
    16–17, 31, 66, 69, 111, 116, 143
architectural history 54, 65, 70–74, 113–114
architectural practice 5
architectural studies courses 58
architectural theories 54–55, 75–77, 113–114
artificial intelligence (AI) 134–136
augmented reality (AR) 133–134
axonometric drawings 43, 121

briefs
    brief writing 87, 118
    final year undergraduate 86–88
    first year undergraduate 35, 45–51
    postgraduate 116–118
    second year undergraduate 63, 64, 66–70
bubble diagrams 87, 121
Building Information Modelling (BIM) 85
building materials 49, 79
building structure 49, 67

carbon footprint 82–85
clearing 28
competitions 100–101
comprehensive design project (CDP) 86
concept diagrams 48–49, 50
continuing professional development (CPD) 154
contracts 118, 153–154
cores 49
credit system 143
critical paths 119–121
critical thinking 88
crits 51–53, 56, 88
CVs 93, 94
cyborgian geography 129

deadlines 59–60
deferrals 98
design projects
    final year undergraduate 86–88
    first year undergraduate 35, 36–37, 45–51
    postgraduate 116–118
    second year undergraduate 63, 64, 66–70
    structure 36–37
    sustainable design 82–85
design studio 35–37, 64, 79
    see also design projects
displacement activity 48, 52, 87
dissertations 86, 121
drawings 40
    axonometric 43, 121
    concept diagrams 48–49, 50

elevations 42, 48, 50
    for first building brief 50–51
    isometric 43
    perspective 43, 50
    plans 40–41, 48, 50, 121
    scale 40, 41
    sections 41–42, 48, 50, 51, 121
    sketches 40, 50–51

elevations 42, 48, 50
emotional problems 60–61
end-of-year shows 8, 56–57, 109
environment and ecology 80
    sustainable design 82–85, 131
equipment lists 28–29
ERASMUS programme 142
essay writing 54–56
ethics 80
external examiners 88, 136–137

financial problems 60
first year undergraduate study 31–61
    briefs 35, 45–51
    course structure 34
    crits 51–53, 56
    design studio 35–37
    drawing, modelling and scaling 40–44,
        50–51
    end-of-year results 57–58
    end-of-year shows 56–57
    essay writing 54–56
    first building proposal 45–51
    lectures 54–55
    mental health 52, 59–61
    options if fail year 57–58
    pastoral care 33, 61
    portfolios 56
    project structure 36–37
    stress management 52, 59–61
    tasks 38–39
foundation programmes **12,** 15–16
full-time study **12–14,** 15

Gantt charts 119–121
GCSEs 6, 26
green design 82–85, 131

history of architecture 54, 65, 70–74, 113–114

interviews 21, 22, 25, 96–98, 108
isometric drawings 43

job applications 93–98, 149
jobs, year-out *see* year-out jobs

league tables 10, 105
lectures 10, 54–55
legal frameworks 118–121
lighting and orientation 47
loans, student 28, 108–109

MArch *see* postgraduate study
materials, building 49, 79
mental health 52, 59–61
mentorship scheme 58
modelling 44, 51

narrative, semiotics and performance 129

office life 99–102
open days 8, 21

Part 1 *see* undergraduate study
Part 2 *see* postgraduate study
Part 3 151–155
part-time study **13–14,** 15, 98, 108
pastoral care 33, 61
PEDR *see* RIBA Professional Experience and
    Development Record (PEDR)
peer-group support 61
perspective drawings 43, 50
Photoshop 44
plans 40–41, 48, 50, 121
portfolios 21–22, 25, 56, 96, 97, 108
post-digital architecture 125–131
postgraduate study 102–109, 111–137
    applications 108–109
    apprenticeships **14,** 103, 106
    architectural speculation 122–125
    artificial intelligence 134–136
    augmented reality 133–134
    briefs 116–118
    course options 102–103, 106–107
    final assessment 136–137
    full-time study 15
    history, theory and futures 113–114
    part-time study 15, 98, 108
    post-digital architecture 125–131
    realising architecture 116–121
    school selection 105
    student loans 108–109
    thesis 102, 111, 121
practice selection 96, 149
professional and legal frameworks 118–121
professional studies advisors (PSAs) 99
projects *see* design projects

reading lists 28
research excellence framework 10
RIBA Chartered Member 154
RIBA Foundation in Architecture **12,** 16
RIBA job board platform 93–94, 149
RIBA Plan of Work 118
RIBA Professional Experience and Development
    Record (PEDR) 99, 118
RIBA Studio **13–14,** 16, 102–103, 106
RIBA validated schools abroad 142
risers 49

scale 40, 41
schedules of accommodation 35, 64, 87
school selection
    postgraduate 105
    studying abroad 142–147
    undergraduate 17–18
scopic regimes 129
second year undergraduate study 63–85
    briefs 63, 64, 66–70
    course structure 64–66
    ethics 80
    history of architecture 65, 70–74
    skills development 66–70
    sustainable design 82–85

INDEX

technology 74, 78–80
    theory of architecture 75–77
sections 41–42, 48, 50, 51, 121
self-critical appraisal 111
sensors 129
service runs 49
site analysis 45, 118
sketches 40, 50–51
social media 8–10, 32
space 39, 129
stress management 52, 59–61
structural systems 49, 67
student loans 28, 108–109
studio 35–37, 64, 79
    see also design projects
studying abroad 105, 141–147
sustainable design 82–85, 131

taster days 8, 21
technology 74, 78–80, 122–125, 129
    artificial intelligence 134–136
    augmented reality 133–134
    ethics 80
    sustainable design 82–85
theory of architecture 54–55, 75–77, 113–114
thesis 102, 111, 121
time, continuum of 129–131
time management 52, 59–60, 63–64, 101
trabeated structural system 49, 67

UCAS 19–21, 26–27, 28
unconditional offers 27
undergraduate application process
    application form 19–21
    clearing 28
    interviews 21, 22, 25
    offers 25, 26–27
    portfolios 21–22, 25
    pre-application research 5–17
    school selection 17–18
    UCAS tariffs 26, 27, 28
    unconditional offers 27
undergraduate study
    alternative routes 15–17, 27
    apprenticeships **13,** 15
    equipment lists 28–29
    final year 86–88
    full-time study **12–14,** 15
    part-time study **13–14,** 15
    programme comparison **12–14**
    reading lists 28
    student loans 28
    see also first year undergraduate study;
    second year undergraduate study
unit' system 34

vanishing points 43

written work
    brief writing 87, 118
    dissertations 86, 121
    essays 54–56
    postgraduate thesis 102, 111, 121

year' system 34

year-out jobs 93–102
    applications 93–98
    competitions 100–101
    CVs 93, 94
    deferrals 98
    interviews 96–98
    office life 99–102
    PEDR 99
    portfolios 96, 97
    practice selection 96
    tasks 99–101
    working abroad 95

Get your Free RIBA Student Membership online today

architecture.com/join-riba/free-student-membership

As a student on a RIBA recognised Part 1 or 2 course, or during your year out between Part 1 and Part 2, you are entitled to FREE RIBA membership.

Growing your network
We can introduce you to a community of architects and other professionals.

Learn from the best
Join over 150,000 people attending our events, exhibitions and talks each year. As a Student Member you get free and discounted tickets.

Exclusive access to funding
We allocate over £200k every year, through our scholarships, bursaries and student support fund.

To find out about all these benefits and more, go to architecture.com/join-riba

Gain insight from architects
Be part of our exclusive student mentoring programme, join more than 1,000 students learning and being inspired by our Chartered Members.

Specialist knowledge, resources, expertise and advice
Our Members Information Service is there to answer any practical or technical queries as well as study and career guidance.

Broadening your knowledge and skills
Take advantage of discounts on all our professional seminars to keep up to date with all the latest architectural developments.

Keep in touch with the RIBA team:

RIBA Membership
Tel: +44 (0)20 7307 3686
Email: membership.development@riba.org

Twitter: @RIBA
Instagram: @RIBA
Facebook: @RIBA